I0591950

CHRONICLES OF CHAOS

CHRONICLES OF CHAOS

2019–2022 A.D.

REV. JUSTIN CRIADO

Chronicles of Chaos: 2019–2022 A.D.
Rev. Justin Criado

Copyright © 2022 by Justin Criado

Previous versions of almost all pieces included within originally appeared in the now-defunct newspaper The Watch and Telluride Daily Planet between July 2019 and June 2022 in the monthly column The Chopping Block.

All rights reserved. No part of this book may be reproduced in any form or by any electronic or mechanical means, including information storage and retrieval systems, without written permission from the author, except for the use of brief quotations in a book review.

Trade Paperback ISBN: 978-0-578-26982-5

Cover art by Gordiart (Instagram: @_gordiart_)

Cover design by Rick Bickhart

Author photo by Mo Pihl

Printed in the USA

For Mum, Dad and Karlee, who all believed in me before I believed in myself. I love you.

CONTENTS

"Try and be alone and not lonely."

— HE IS LEGEND, "THAT'S NASTY"

PEACOCKS AND PAIN

Dentists are terrifying. They're up there with clowns, spiders and scorned women when it comes to everyday horrors. I'm convinced anyone who makes a living mining mouths, picking and prodding the face's exposed bits of bones, is some type of sociopath.

Willy Wonka's dentist dad screwed him up for life by strapping unnecessary headgear on him at an early age and burning all his Halloween candy so he wouldn't get cavities. But instead of locking 'em up and reforming them for orally mutilating innocent people, we actually pay to see a dentist in America.

Growing up, I looked forward to visiting the dentist. My teeth were always clean, if not falling out, and my dentist had a treasure chest full of toys to pick from after a successful checkup. The presents weren't anything fancy but walking out of the dentist's office blowing on a brand new blue plastic kazoo gave a kid a sense of accomplishment. My mouth passed inspection, my tune said. Next time I could grab myself a mood ring or a temporary skull and crossbones tattoo. Oral hygiene had its perks, I learned at a young age.

I even had an extra baby tooth surgically removed as an

eight-year-old, which resulted in stitches and braces for several weeks until the gap in my smile closed. It's disgusts me now to think that my tender juvenile gums needed to be cut open so a tooth that shouldn't have been there could be extracted. Retained deciduous teeth are a common occurrence in cats and dogs. Too bad I'm not a polyphyodont. Sharks and crocodiles have all the luck sometimes. But I remember the dentist recommended ice cream as a pain reliever. I can still taste the strawberry milkshake and blood from that first post-surgery meal.

These thoughts came to me before a recent visit to the local dentist. Scheduled for a routine six-month cleaning, the nerves started a couple days beforehand. I found myself standing in front of my bathroom mirror, stretching my lips as wide as possible, in search of problem spots for hours. My gums are receding, and I'm not even 30, I thought. This can't be good. Wiggling one tooth at a time, I thought about forcibly pulling them out like I do in most of my dreams and opting for dentures. Freud thought dreams about tooth extraction equaled sexual repression. Other mystics believe it has something to do with fear of aging, struggles with acceptance or lack of assertiveness. Or maybe it's just good old fashioned self-mutilation. Solid foods are overrated anyway, but not all of us are lucky enough to turn into humanoid flies that can vomit stomach acid onto food and don't need teeth anymore, like Jeff Goldblum in David Cronenberg's 1986 remake of "The Fly."

But I bought a new toothbrush in anticipation of my visit, one that supposedly cleans gums and tongues better, according to the marketing blurb on the packaging, and scrubbed my mouth raw for a week. My teeth stayed in their proper places. My gums bled less. Even my tongue looked healthy.

Then it was time to see if any of my efforts made a difference, as the day of reckoning came. I walked the short distance across town from my apartment, as the winter weather made my breath visible along the way. A visit to the dentist isn't supposed to feel like a death-row shuffle to the electric chair, but I couldn't help but imagine settling into the padded recliner only to be unexpectedly strapped in and electrocuted. Executioners have found at least 2,000 volts of electricity at 12 amps for 30 seconds will kill a person. Dentists aren't good with numbers. They judge voltage by how fast a person's eyeballs fly out of their skull. At least criminal institutions tape the peepers shut.

A deranged dentist with a blood-splattered electric saw would be my last vision before I succumbed to the fatal current. The mad tooth torturer could have their way with me after that, and not only with my mouth. I shuddered at the thought of being molested by my dentist, but I continued toward the office anyway, which is tucked away in a nondescript row of rented storefronts on the first floor of a condo complex. What a perfect place for such a sadist to hide. No one would suspect anything out of the ordinary with an office between a day care and hair spa. The tenants above the office may wonder about the faint smells of burning meat from time to time, but other than that, it's a great location and place to live.

I walked through the door and into the small waiting room, which featured outdated magazines on a small coffee table and walls covered with tacky posters about the benefits of clean teeth.

I exchanged pleasantries with the lady at the front desk, a zombie of a person who no doubt exchanged her soul for perfectly straight teeth and health insurance. She asked for my name. I thought about giving an alias, as if it would have saved me from the impending face fisting.

" ... Justin."

"Oh, yes, we have you here," the zombie with a Crest smile said as she scanned the computer in front of her. "Have a seat, and we'll call you back when we're ready." When they're ready. They never ask if you are or not.

Would she also have a turn shoving her fingers into my mouth while I lay there unconscious? What does she know? My mind began to race. I picked up a back issue of *Sports Illustrated Kids* with quarterback Cam Newton on the cover. Now there's a million-dollar smile. Wonder what he had to go through to get it.

As I daydreamed about Newton's mouth, a faceless dentist in scrubs called me into the back. We made small talk as she walked me to the chair, but I knew she only wanted to assuage my hesitancy before putting me in a vulnerable position.

I sat and settled into the chair without a second thought, before the dentist leaned it back. The mechanical hum of the torture device straightening out reminded me that such executioners charge up and test the vitality of the electrical current before an execution. Is that what took them so long to call me back?

The cleaning began once I was horizontal. The high-pitched squeal of the apparatus scraping against my teeth gave me goosebumps. I watched for any quick movements out of the corner of my eye. If they were going to knock me out and fondle me, they were going to get a fight first. When the power tool in my mouth hit sensitive spots, I gripped the leather armrests and focused on the flatscreen TV bolted to the ceiling above me.

An image of a colorful peacock in full bloom caught my attention. What a beautiful creature, I thought, but when you associate them with dental duress, they become mocking monsters. Peacocks don't have to worry about bad teeth or rotting gums as they flaunt about with their skinny necks and butts full of feathers.

I began to envy their beaks. Lying there, I convinced myself that I could survive on a diet of bugs and berries. Somedays I may even catch a newt to nibble on. I'd never have to see a dentist again, I imagined as the screen quickly flashed to another image.

Cute cartoons of molars fighting off blackened troglodytes displayed dental fun facts about tooth plaque and periodontal disease. The molars were big and burly, like body builders, while the cavity critters were gnarled and devious looking. If this was supposed to make children feel better about their little kissers, then dentists have a sicker sense of humor than I initially thought.

Then there were the close-up pictures of mouths. Lying on your back as a stranger operates a dental drill in your mouth, while before and after pictures of crooked smiles and stained teeth are displayed on the screen is some type of torture. It's like a scene out of "Hostel." The only thing worse would be a live feed of the cleaning to accompany the coppery taste of blood, which eventually began to collect at the back of my throat. I started to choke, and the urge to cough it up became undeniable. My eyes started to water, and I couldn't believe these bastards got me right where they wanted me without so much as a flinch.

But before I could throw a punch across my body at the tooth taker's temple, the faceless dentist shoved a tube at my uvula and sucked up the liquid. I began to breathe easier, but it didn't end my agony. I waited for an oral fisting, as I continued to focus on the TV above me.

Between the peacocks and chipped teeth, photos of staff would come up every so often. I couldn't help but look at their perfect grins. The smiles reminded me of the saying that beauty is pain, then a shiver ran through my body as the cleaning apparatus found a nerve ending near my gum line, and I realized you don't have to be beautiful to experience pain, at least not in the dentist's chair.

I could feel the tears drying at the corners of my eyes. I adjusted to swallowing my blood and phlegm in short, quick gulps. At a certain point, I gave in and embraced it, almost enjoyed it. *Am I a sadist, too? Could I finger a stranger's mouth, bloody gums and all? How much force does it take to pull out a healthy tooth?* The pain and perverted pleasures of a dentist visit are always temporary, but a pretty smile lasts a little longer.

After almost an hour of fondling my mouth, the peacock popped up on the TV again with its colored feathers and toothless black beak. Damn, rainbow goose. Then the pain stopped. Feeling relieved and violated, I checked out with the zombie at the front desk and agreed to return in six months.

HANGOVERS AND
HEAVY METAL

There's something about cheap beer that makes me happy. Maybe it's habit. Maybe it's the effect. Maybe it's both. I've learned alcoholism is funny like that. One moment you're enjoying a crisp cold one and the next you're sick as a rat with a belly full of Raid, praying to some type of higher power and swearing you'll never ingest the stuff again if you manage to survive this purge. It's a small price to pay. The gods haven't killed me off yet, so I take it as some sort of sign of strength and perseverance. But the same can be said about a cockroach.

My all-time favorite beer is Iron City bottles, or Pittsburgh Pabst, as I call it. It goes down easy. Too easy, most of the time. As a registered minister of the Universal Life Church Monastery, which I'm convinced gives me some credit with the powers that be, my friends had me officiate their Friday the 13th wedding a couple years ago. My payment? A case of Iron City bottles. The lord works in mysterious ways. It's a shame it's not sold west of the Ohio River.

I refer to myself as a budget beer connoisseur. Historically, I've sipped on Pabst Blue Ribbon, which was voted America's best beer in 1893, as the can still proudly states. That's the same year Chicago hosted the World's Columbian Exposition to celebrate the 400th anniversary of Christopher Columbus's arrival. A grand event by all accounts, but the history books leave out one of the most exciting aspects of the celebration.

Local entrepreneur H.H. Holmes built an apartment complex in the city shortly before the world's fair, which became a popular spot during the event, though for sinister reasons. Guests checked in, but never checked out. Holmes, who had a medical background, became what many consider America's first serial killer, as he dismembered people in macabre ways. Leaking poisonous gas through the vents allowed him to rack up the kills, before having fun with his guest's bodies. Vats of acid in the basement made disposal more efficient and less wasteful. His building earned the nickname the "Murder Castle." It got terrible Yelp reviews. There are theories that Holmes also may have doubled as the infamous international murderer Jack the Ripper, who terrorized the streets of London from 1888 to 1891, as a handful of long-lost documents point to Holmes potentially being in Whitechapel during the timeframe of widespread bloodshed. The law eventually caught up to Holmes, and he was hung in Philadelphia in 1896, a short time after Pabst reached the pinnacle of brewing excellence.

Every time I order a Pabst and see that "Selected as America's Best in 1893" proclamation, I think of Mr. Holmes. The lord works in mysterious ways.

Here in Telluride, my go-to swill is the $2 Utica Club cans that O'Bannon's Pub serves up. The bartenders there know to garnish it with a lime wedge. I'm classy, after all. But boozing alone like Bukowski is a sure sign of alcoholism, which is why I won't do it, so I like to share happy hour and late nights with like-minded friends, especially at the end of a long week, or a random weeknight, that spirals into revelry. The kind that ends with you praying and hugging a toilet.

The boys know how to have a good time ... aka we drink heavily and listen to heavy metal. The ritual is surely terrifying to the outsiders. If witnessing drunken displays of unfounded confidence wasn't bad enough, imagine the scene having a soundtrack featuring distorted guitars and double-bass drums.

It's not a proper night out if Judas Priest's "Thunder Road" isn't blared through OB's fuzzy speakers, while we all strike power poses and play air guitar like hairy, overgrown 12-year-olds with rockstar aspirations. But this is America, and if you want to get drunk in public and mimic Rob Halford's high-pitched pipes with your buddies, have at it.

On any given night, the playlist may also include Ratt ("Round and Round"), W.A.S.P. ("I Wanna Be Somebody"), David Lee Roth ("Just Like Paradise"), Dokken ("Breaking the Chains"), Skid Row ("Slave to the Grind") and anything Van Halen (not Van Hagar), among other bangers. These are bands that had their heyday during the hair metal boom of the 1980s. The guitar licks and solos are over the top, the lyrics are cheesy as hell but anthemic, and we look like fools imitating them.

If we want to get more technical with our barroom musicianship, we'll throw on some heavier stuff — Slayer, Metallica, Motorhead — and hope we don't get forearm cramps feigning triplets. Our one buddy, we'll call him Shane, is a drummer, so he air drums, while the rest of us play lead. We all handle vocal duties, but nobody wants to play air bass. Shit, no one wants to play bass in real life either.

Sometimes I'll put on some Killswitch Engage, Mastodon or He Is Legend. It doesn't go over well with my fellow head-bangers. One particular bartender, who shall remain nameless, skips those types of "screamer" songs. And absolutely no Lamb of God, the bartender reminds me every time I'm standing in front of the jukebox, swaying and unsteady. The bartender created the unwritten rule after I took advantage of the free plays available during weekday happy hours one too many times. The bartender, who has a reputation of being a pain in the ass and will no sooner tell a person off than listen to Lamb of God, became enraged whenever Randy Blythe's vocals came on.

"Who played this shit?" the bartender would always bark.

She looked like Tank Girl and had the attitude to match.

I'd bashfully admit to pressing play on "Walk With Me In Hell."

"I can't stand this fuckin' shit," and the bartender would skip to the next song, every time.

Well, I've never been one to take a hint, so I made a habit of playing at least one Lamb of God song every time the bartender worked weekday happy hour shifts. It became too hard to hide at a certain point, so I'd been informed to never play Lamb of God during her shifts again, which I respected. But she never said I couldn't play Deicide.

Through such antics at OB's, I met friends with similar musical tastes, which only evolved into impromptu head-banging at the bar and sideways looks from uninterested women.

But all anyone ever asks of us during this public display of insanity is we headbang away from the uninterested, if not confused, patrons and leave when the clock strikes 2 a.m. Even then, we usually spill into the street, light up American Spirits and stumble to someone's house in order to keep the party going. Naturally, these private events include more metal, air shredding and libations.

If you've never drank aged Armenian brandy out of a machine gun-shaped bottle while blaring Black Sabbath, then you haven't lived life to its fullest. But this is our communion. A shared interest in good times and metal music is what brought us together.

The first time I met my friend John we ended up back at his place quizzing each other about Slayer albums and throwing down to "Raining Blood" and "God Hates Us All." The lord works in mysterious ways.

John's a quiet guy who rarely shows much emotion when he's sober, but get a couple beers in him, and he'll high kick and rock out with the best of them. His mom and aunt both dated David Lee Roth in high school back in California, so we have a running joke that David Lee Roth is his daddy. He doesn't necessarily deny it either, and he can hit those trademark David Lee Roth high notes pretty well.

At some point during every late-night jam session, we make plans to start our own band. It's going to be a blend of metal, punk, grindcore and surf rock. We're still pondering the name, and Shane needs to go to the Front Range to get his drums — something he's been meaning to do for the past three years. John has the guitars and a bass, and we'll all sing, because we all have different vocal strengths.

As another friend Stan put it one night, "I just want to make music that scares people." We all snickered in agreement, then cracked another beer and turned up Iron Maiden. Bruce Dickinson screamed, "I have a constant fear that something's always near. Fear of the dark! Fear of the dark!"

MAGPIES AND MURDER

A *sparrow sits on the railing outside my window twitching its head spastically. It's raining, and I wonder if birds have eyelids. The same bird has visited me every morning around the same time for the past month. I'm beginning to think we're friends. Should I give it a name? No, birds don't need names.*

I wrote this silly note during the summer — nearly two months before I witnessed a murder out of the same office window my avian companion and I often had our visits at. It's been hard to shake. Such a gruesome act sticks with a man.

One morning in early fall, as I was waiting for my feathered friend to arrive for our dawn pleasantries, a loud bang shocked my coworker Suzanne Cheavens and me from our work.

People who are more in tune with the universe than I am believe a bird flying into a window in front of you is a precursor to your death. Death erases student loan and credit card debt, at least. The act can also symbolize some type of ending in your life — a relationship, a difficult phase, a hangover. The most logical explanation is birds see the reflection of the outdoors in the window and, you know, don't even know what a window is.

But if I die soon, I blame the building's maintenance crew for my untimely demise for cleaning the windows so well.

Some brown-and-white feathers and a smudged outline were left behind on the glass from the sudden impact, then I saw it. There, on the ledge below the railing, my birdie lay on its back, panting. He seemed to be paralyzed, as only his tiny eyes and breast moved, but he was alive and breathing, though clearly struggling. I should have trusted my instincts and jumped out of the window immediately to save him, for what followed will remain in my mind forever.

Shortly after the crash, a magpie perched itself on the railing above my dying friend.

"He's thinking about breakfast," Suzanne said.

"What? Birds eat birds? Like cannibals?" I wondered.

I again thought about jumping out of the window and staving off the bloodthirsty magpie. I could nurse birdie back to health, I thought, even if I had to make him a special wheelchair or tape his head back on. Pretty bird, pretty bird. But nature runs its course, with or without human intervention. It happened so fast I barely noticed. The magpie murderer was on top of birdie, plucking the feathers from his chest in small tufts, faster than I could comprehend. Birdie may have been screaming, but I couldn't hear anything.

Then the killer threw birdie onto the sidewalk and finished the job. Like I said, gruesome. I joked that avian cannibalism is pretty metal, but I was shocked and heartbroken.

Two other coworkers who overheard my panic came to the window to watch the magpie murder. We chatted casually about the cruelty of Mother Nature. None of us have ever witnessed a train wreck, but we agreed we were under a similar spell that day.

"It's like I can't not watch," one coworker commented.

"I hate this," I said.

The magpie left birdie's head and feet, the least digestible parts, lying there on the road. But the smell of blood still hung in the air, as a tiding of magpies gathered at the scene and disposed of the rest of the carcass. One grabbed its feet. Another had the head in its mouth and flew to a nearby fence post to feast.

One mangy looking character poked its head into my open window and pecked at the papers on the edge of my desk before I shooed it away. No magpie is going to kill my friend in front of me and then have the audacity to mock me.

I became more enraged than logically necessary, and I wanted revenge. God knows what I would have done if that malnourished trash bat — it was molting, as Suzanne explained to me — came within my grasp. Images of Ozzy Osbourne biting the head off of a dove came to mind. I'd teach the magpie killers a lesson in violence. My coworkers, who quickly lost interest in the whole spectacle, would have no other choice but to call the police after I started chewing the heads off of magpies and screeching in retribution. I'd tear my clothes off and use the dead birds' blood to stick feathers to myself. Incensed and grieving, I'd have to be gunned down in the street, no doubt, but at least I'd be with birdie.

After the initial excitement of the kill died down and everyone returned to their desks, I continued to watch the crime scene and mourned. Birdie's gone. Several magpies late to the party hung around the sidewalk and railing area as if they were waiting for a second course to be served.

Then the ravens arrived. There they are, I thought. The raven has always been my spirit animal, more so a guardian and undeniable proof that the universe always balances itself out. I can't properly explain it, but I've had numerous encounters with ravens throughout my life that were too spiritual to simply be considered coincidences. I feel that they watch over me, to a degree, and welcome me wherever I go. For example, when I moved into my new condo recently, I was unpacking my truck when a caw caught my attention. I turned toward the sound, and there on the complex's roof above my unit sat a raven. "Hello, friend," I whispered.

People think I'm screwy when I tell them such tales, but there's a reason I have two raven tattoos scarred into my flesh forever. At least ravens are physical, breathing creatures and not some amorphous spirit hiding in the clouds who uses fire and famine to teach humans, a species created in this god's image, moral lessons about butt sex and proper parenting.

After birdie's demise, the magpies were manic to satiate their blood lust. The ravens surrounded the magpies on the railing and sidewalk, but didn't confront them. The conspiracy of ravens was restoring order to my world. They must have sensed my pain and confusion. I gave them a head nod as a "thank you."

Humans are mowing each other down with machine guns every day, while birds peck each other to death. Goddamn, I thought, this world is a mad place to make it. The incident only further proved that I'm ignorant to the ways of the world, but I still miss my birdie.

EPILOGUE: An ex, who I have been cursed to run into every now and then around town, read this piece and had the audacity to say it made her cry because it was about her. I used to call her Pretty Bird, after we watched the movie "Dumb and Dumber" together and laughed at the scene of a blind kid petting a decapitated parakeet named Petey that Jim Carrey's character Lloyd sold to him for some quick cash. "Pretty bird, pretty bird," the blind child said as he petted Petey. Caught off guard by her narcissistic assumption, I didn't have the wit in that moment to spit back that she was always more of a snake than a pretty bird. If only her head would fall off.

FEAR FESTERS

There's a standard dictionary definition of "fear" that anyone can look up. It would be a waste of time and space to include it here. The sources of it are different, but everyone knows what fear feels like. Some of us experience it more often than others.

Growing up, I was afraid of my own shadow. Everything scared me. From severe storm warnings flashing across the bottom of the TV screen to potential alien invasions, I lived in what felt like a constant state of fear, ready to run from whatever catastrophe life chose to throw at me. That's to say I was Chuckie Finster, basically. Only later on did I realize my doomsday mental state, which I've become better at quelling, is called anxiety, which has saved me from a lifelong panic attack.

It didn't help that my older cousins deliberately frightened me with scary movies, mainly "It," during those fragile years. I can remember seeing Tim Curry's Pennywise for the first time more vividly than most of my childhood memories. My younger sister Karlee and I were at Grandma's house with my three cousins — Jason, Lindsay and Matt, who were all siblings.

We were watching TV in Grandma's basement living room

when "It" came on. My cousins already knew about it because they were old enough to know things like that. They also knew that it'd frighten their skittish baby cousin. Reflecting on it now, I can't think of a clown before Pennywise unexpectedly crashed into my psyche. I told them to stop, to change the channel. Grandma always watched the soap opera "Days of Our Lives," and I found the introduction soothing. "Like sands through the hourglass, so are the days of our lives." I suggested that, but my cousins giggled and turned up the volume. My sister, who couldn't have been more than five years old, sat there unphased, which only convinced my baby brain that Pennywise wanted me and only me.

He could turn fortune cookies into oozing orifices and lives in a complex sewer system only he knows how to efficiently navigate. I'd never be able to escape if he dragged me to his underground kingdom. He'd chew on my spindly limbs like chicken wings. Poor Georgie. I felt his fear. My panic blurs what happened next that fateful day at Grandma's, but an adult stepped in to stop my torture. It didn't matter. The damage had been done. I avoided clowns for over a decade. They still irk me.

In Pittsburgh, there used to be a steamboat called the Good Ship Lollipop that trolled the city's three rivers with its crew of clowns. They'd welcome kids to join them to experience downtown from a different point of view, but I always knew they were lying. That it had to be a trap. Why couldn't the adults see that such a carnival cruise was a ruse to drag their children to the lawlessness of international waters where the clowns could do whatever they wanted with us? For all I knew, Pennywise had christened the Good Ship Lollipop the flagship of his demon fleet. I don't know if the ship is still in service, but if it is I have half a mind to sink it. May it rest and rot away at the bottom of the Monongahela River. No child would ever again have to endure the weirdness of it all. The giant catfish of local lore would make quick work of the clowns. But Pennywise still occasionally visits me in my dreams.

I took the opportunity to pass down the fear years later when I let my younger cousin Joe watch the original "Pet Semetary." The scenes of the bedridden Zelda and undead Victor made him visibly uncomfortable, but he continued to act tough and sit through it. I have to give him credit. He took it better than I had.

But once Gage died and came back as a demon child, Joe couldn't handle it any longer. My uncle stormed in after Gage hid under the bed, sliced poor Jud's Achilles tendon and then bit his throat for a bloody kill. "OK, that's enough," he said, and the party was over.

My dad, who hated when I'd complain about on-screen horrors, would constantly tell me how fake it all was.

"Imagine all the bloopers of them laughing," he'd say. But I couldn't. Clowns ate children since the beginning of time, and baby dolls were alive and liked to kill kids with kitchen knives. These were facts of life. He didn't get it.

It's ironic that I grew to love scary movies, but I still don't do haunted houses or any other fake frights. The real world has always provided me with enough scares on a daily basis. Or spiders. Never had an affinity for those eight-legged freaks with their head full of eyes, bulbous butts that poop out sticky webs, and their uncanny ability to pop out at just the right time, like when you're in the shower or on the pot, immobilized and vulnerable. Tarantulas supposedly taste like popcorn if you fry them over a fire. I learned that from one of those backcountry survival shows. But you have to cook them just right, or they'll fuck up your stomach. It's something with the boiling point of their venom. I'd rather eat my own arm or starve to death. But I digress.

It's Halloween, and everyone's feeling spooky. How cute. It's a holiday that has become associated with free candy, elaborate costumes and pumpkin carving, but its origins are more fantastical. About 2,000 years ago in modern-day Ireland, Britain and northern France, the Celts celebrated their Nov. 1 new year with a festival the night of Oct. 31 called Samhain. The revelers would dress up and dance around bonfires lit with crops and sacrificial animals. It was a time when the Druids, Celtic priests and prophets looked into the future, hoping for good fortune during the upcoming harvest. They also believed the dead returned to Earth around the same time to terrorize the living. The ritual slaughters and willingness to burn their crops was meant to appease the restless spirits. This tradition continued until the Roman Empire conquered the Celtic territories around 43 A.D. Samhain then cross-pollinated with similar Roman fall festivals, including All Saints' Day and All Souls' Day on Nov. 1 and Nov. 2, respectively. The night before All Saints' Day was eventually called All Hallows' Eve or Halloween (it was still Samhain, if you were Celtic).

Halloween didn't catch on right away in the newly established American colonies, given the power of the Protestant religion. Colonials would hold harvest festivals each fall, but Halloween wasn't widely accepted or celebrated until more Europeans immigrated to America. It's morphed into what it is today after centuries of reinterpretation, barely resembling the original incarnation. Nowadays, especially in America, Samhain is more associated with Glenn Danzig's deathrock band of the same name after he left the Misfits or the movie "The Wicker Man."

Like the Celts' Samhain festival, words have a way of redefining themselves over time. To me, fear isn't Tim Curry in clown makeup anymore, though I'm still terrified of having my Achilles cut whenever I sit on the edge of my bed.

I'll let Kurt Vonnegut explain, as he did in a 1978 letter to his daughter Nanny: "About fear: I heard a Hindu holy man say at a lecture a couple years ago that it was crucial to learn how to make decisions without allowing fear to become involved — and that fear liked to hitch rides on all sorts of words and images. When fear intrudes on your thinking, it may be an old, old fear, hitching a ride still, but one which need not really concern you anymore."

Fear for me is more of an internal creation now; it's insidious, hitching a ride on my insecurities and paranoia. Fear festers inside my skull. It's inaction, more than anything — a frequent feeling of inadequacy or complacency. Fear is self-doubt. Fear is regret. Fear is caring what other people think of you. Fear is letting free will slip away. Fear is a façade you create that hides what you truly want to do and say. Fear is faking it. Fear is wasting time. Fear is man-made. Ultimately, fear is a mythical hitchhiker, but we all still feel it catching a ride on everyday trivialities, some more than others.

DECADENCE AND DECAY

A lot goes through the mind of someone on the verge of completing another decade on Earth. There are generalized notions that certain periods of life are more raucous than others, while many believe the more decades one accrues means more wisdom and leisure.

I recently turned 29. On the eve of 30, my early 20s, particularly after I turned 21, were filled with late nights drinking and hanging out with motorcycle gangs. Sleep became more of a burden than anything, which is to say I didn't get much of it and maximized each day's 24 hours by staying awake for most of them. Drinks, debauchery, women, work. Late nights turned into early mornings that blurred into more late nights.

My blooming body handled the stress and damage admirably, but with each passing year, the recovery time lengthened, until slowing down or dying seemingly became the only two options to surviving the great disintegration.

Yes, 29 is one year less alive, but still young. I know this, but my body's unwillingness to cooperate with the day-to-day rigors of existence hasn't validated it. I celebrated my recent birthday by going to the doctor and being reminded I'm still overweight, which I've been since birth (I was a 10-plus-pound baby), and going blind. I also knew this, but the old eyeballs are drying out quicker than I've realized.

The dread of a visit to the doctor only increases as the years do. More pills are pushed on you to numb the mind and keep everything working properly, at least physically. I take pride in the fact that I don't have to swallow meds to get through the day, but that's the Western way. Prozac, Zoloft and Xanax make for a balanced American breakfast, followed by servings of OxyContin and Percocet to round out a standard daily diet. This sad reality is evident in overdose deaths and addiction statistics.

I told myself before my visit that I would not give them too much information, particularly about my mental state and constant anxiety that often physically manifests itself in a tightening chest and tingling legs. At this age, I'd rather feel everything existence has to offer me than subdue it. There is a bluntness about the sobriety of being alive that I enjoy. I've tried to mask it through the alternative methods of excessive alcohol consumption, experimenting with drugs and meaningless sex, but that's cheating, I began telling myself. Don't give them too much, Justin.

The poor physician's assistant, God bless her, who walked me through the initial steps of my physical had me read the eye chart in the hallway first. With both eyes, I could barely see the third line. I mumbled some shapes — "Uh, three bars, a star and a heart" — that were actually supposed to be letters.

"Try again," she said.

"Um, holy hell, E, A, M."

Then we did one eye at a time. I could only read the top line. You know, the one that has two letters the size of saucers.

"F, P," I said with some sort of pride, but I was embarrassed. "It's been over a year since I've seen the eye doctor."

"Maybe you should go soon," she said with sincerity, but I sensed the pity. How does someone so blind even get dressed in the morning, she must have thought. A friend recently suggested Lasik, or laser eye surgery, but that's terrifying. Laser eye surgery sounds like a type of torture employed on the Death Star. I'll stick with wearing magnifying lenses on my face.

Driving at night without glasses has become a public health concern, as I can barely see the front of my hood, let alone pedestrians. Wildlife darting out onto the blacktop? Forget it. Instant roadkill.

Then there's strolling the sidewalks and walking past people I know.

"I saw you at the post office the other day."

"Really? Did I have my glasses on?"

"No."

"Then I didn't see you. Sorry."

My lack of vision has also made me obtuse to any nonverbal communication, especially provocative cues through the din of a bar.

"Dude, she's been looking at you."

"Why?"

"I don't know. She seems into you."

"Why?"

"Jesus. Are you blind?"

"Yes."

"Just go over there."

If I do take a third party's word for it, then I must first apologize for literally not seeing them. By then, the magic and intrigue are gone. The moment's passed, and I return to my drink no better or worse.

Speaking of drinking, my triglycerides are high, which essentially means my blood is also overweight.

"How often do you drink?" the doctor asked.

"Uh, usually just on the weekends. Friday, Saturday, Sunday ... sometimes Thursday. Maybe a Monday here or there. But I don't necessarily get hammered every time I go out to drink."

"How much do you drink when you do?"

"Several."

"Well, high triglycerides means too many carbs, and all alcohol, especially beer, is a big one. Practicing moderation is important."

I know this, too, but I'm terribly impressionable sometimes when it comes to peer pressure. Doc explained that consuming more than two 12-ounce beers per session is considered binge drinking. I then admitted I'm a binge drinker.

Plus, if the triglycerides get too high, pancreatitis is a threat. Thanks to Google, I learned that means the pancreas basically tries to digest itself, which is "very painful" and often requires hospitalization for several days, doc further explained. My liver quivered. I will never touch booze again, my brain said. Putting less alcohol into my body will also lower my uric acid levels, meaning I will have fewer gout bouts.

Lord knows a gout flair up makes a man consider amputation. Every time my feet and ankles swell, I think about that scene from "Saw." You know, the one the whole franchise is named after, when the guy with his ankle shackled to a pipe is given a handsaw in order to free himself by, well, you get it. At least my situation is not life or death, just pain relief.

The degenerate drunk early 20s version of myself gifted me a gout diagnosis last year, complete with regular blood tests. The procedure always makes me nervous and nauseous. Don't eat anything within 12 hours of the test and drink a lot of water so your veins are as thick and juicy as earthworms, they tell me. But the physician's assistant never taps a vein on the first shot, so I sit there like a human pin cushion with sweaty palms and a frantic heartbeat trying not pass out. I can't look, but there's no way to not know where they're puncturing the skin. They typically tap my wrists and the fleshy creases inside my arms. But sometimes they've had to hit the back of my hand and even in between my fingers. At least I'll never pick up heroin.

Gout is called the "disease of kings" since it was most associated with overindulgence during medieval times. Can you imagine a fat-footed king gnawing on wild boar, while watching knights joust, guffawing and carrying on among the peasants? Man, times were simpler. Gout was a status symbol back then. Now you're a sloven. Too much drink. Too much red meat. Too much seafood. Too much too much. The pills are starting to sound like a good substitute. Maybe doc could prescribe me a beer-drinking tapeworm.

My daydream ended when doc said they'd like to test my blood again in a couple months. Instead of putting my foot down and telling him off — "Let me perish in peace, goddamitt!" — I just nodded in agreement.

We are all sacks of expiring meat. We become fat and flabby, gaseous and gangrenous, dried out and dead. Slowly we rot. Sorry if that sounds so somber. It's not a case of Cotard's syndrome, just a fact of nature. I actually enjoy my life on this dying planet — vanishing vision, expanding waistline and all. Here's to cutting out those carbs.

PITTSBURGH

Everything everyone loves and loathes about me is
Pittsburgh. My blue-collar work ethic, my willingness
to help out however I can, my tendency to let people
know where they stand, for better or worse, my sardonic
sarcasm. What you see is what you get. To put it another way:
my best friend, who I've known since kindergarten, calls me
blunt and abrasive. He says if you didn't know me, you'd think
I'm an asshole, but I'm really a big teddy bear. Those are his
words, but I guess he's right. It's really not for me to say or care
about.

To be fair, I grew up in Elizabeth, Pennsylvania, a borough
on the Monongahela River less than 20 miles south of Pittsburgh proper, as the crow flies. Its only claim to fame is that
Lewis and Clark bought one of their boats there before
exploring the land acquired in the Louisiana Purchase. When I
was growing up, the former boat-making business was a bar,
The Shamrock, that served teenagers. Probably still does.

A hooker the townsfolk nicknamed "Whorey Lori" walked a
particular stretch of busy roadway. No one knows exactly how
long she'd been at it, but my parents seemed to remember her

from their high school days. If that's the case, she had to be around 50 years old by the time I became aware of her profession. She looked like it, too. I can't recall the details of her face, but a ghost of who she was haunts the back of my mind. Her clothes were always tattered and dirty, and she never wore shoes. She'd smoke long cigarettes and walked as if one leg was shorter than the other. Lord knows the interactions she had with desperate passersby.

With aliens like Whorey Lori roaming about, Elizabeth might as well have been Mars. Everyone my age seemed to reproduce with each other before they could legally drink. All the schools I attended were next to farms, including the corn-field across from the high school football stadium that was used for parking on Friday nights.

A porno shop was the longest-running business in town. Probably still is. Since they never carded anyone, my friends and I used to get bored and wander in there and giggle at all the sex toys, especially the dildos. There were deep purple dildos and jet-black dildos. There were dildos so big we'd wonder who would want to shove a dildo that size inside themselves. There were dildos so small we'd wonder who would want to shove a dildo that size inside themselves. But people in Elizabeth, Pennsylvania, apparently do.

As we matured, the definition of a good time meant drinking moonshine — that's what we called all homemade grain liquor, but it wasn't quite high-proof ethanol or else we'd all be blind or dead — and getting drunk around a bonfire. We'd built a fire ring in my friend's backyard — about 50 yards from his parent's house in the woods. Seemingly every week-end, we'd steal some beers from his dad's mini-fridge in the garage. His neighbor would come over with a jar of moonshine. He'd explain the different flavors. It'd be apple pie sometimes or black cherry now and then, but it always tasted like lighter fluid. We'd share drinks around a fire. We'd get drunk, or at least act like it, and laugh about high school drama like dildos and prom dates. We didn't get much play in high school.

After graduating, if you cared enough to get a diploma, you started working. College was for cake-eaters, but I saw it as an opportunity to finally leave Elizabeth. A football scholarship helped. I always felt alien in my hometown, like I was too big for such a podunk town. I was going to be somebody. They'd write my name in local history books and name a small rural park after me. There's something to be said for ambition, or ignorance, but I can't say what.

I wanted to flee to a faraway place where no one knew my name, partially because the people in Elizabeth didn't feel like my people. I refused to settle in that decaying part of the country, so I made my way to the Colorado Rockies.

But as the years passed, my Pittsburgh roots have become more evident, especially since I'm so far from home. I now take a certain amount of pride in where I came from and how I grew up. It was salt-of-the-earth, honest living. I've come to see that it ain't like that for everyone everywhere.

That's part of the reason why I still fly the Pittsburgh colors, no matter where I'm at. Even if they've never been there, when people see my Pirates hat or Steelers jacket, they know what it stands for. It's a no-nonsense, work-hard-play-hard sensibility. We take care of our own. Like Charlie Daniels said, "You just go and lay your hand on a Pittsburgh Steelers fan, and I think you're gonna finally understand."

Enough time has passed to soften any sour memories and unjustified resentment, and I find myself going home for the holidays more often. It's always a time spent with family and friends, visiting old stomping grounds, and reminiscing, even though it's not the same place I left. The Steel City, which saw numerous steel mills shutter in the 1980s, has undergone a Rust

Belt revival recently as tech has become a booming industry, but she still has her scars and never-say-die character.

I miss Primanti Brothers sandwiches and Iron City beer, tailgating on the North Side during Steelers games, Attic Records in Millvale, and the view of downtown from Mount Washington, to name a few things.

I'll never miss Pittsburgh traffic, though. The numerous tunnels and bridges in and out of the city makes driving feel like a real-life game of Mario Kart. I'm a pretty easygoing guy, but stick me in Pittsburgh's rush hour traffic and I'm liable to snap, stomping across the hoods and roofs of cars, smashing windshields with my fists, and climbing to the highest point nearby with a hostage on my hip. I've been meaning to ask my friend in urban planning how the hell traffic still happens despite our brightest minds continuously working toward building the city of tomorrow. Is it just chalked up to chance, or is it an accepted outcome like typos are for writers? At least typos don't lead to mayhem and aneurysms. Well, maybe sometimes.

Anyway, another year comes to a close as I write this, and it'll be nice to again share it with loved ones back home.

As for my end-of-year thoughts this time around, here it is: It's been a decade of dead ends and deterrents, broken hearts and brain farts. Thank Lemmy it's all in the past.

To think, I'll be 40 by the end of the next decade. A friend told me that your late 20s and early 30s is an important time in figuring out who you truly are in accordance with the planetary alignment and stars. I told her that those stars she bases her life around have most likely been dead for longer than she's been alive, and we're just down here creating some sort of meaning out of the night sky's nonsense in acting like we can read the stars' twinkling shadows, but I understood her point.

WAX ADDICT

S aving money is hard when you have an addiction as severe as mine. Paydays turn into shopping sprees. The bank account seemingly never recovers to previous semi-prosperous levels. You spend hours online searching the web for deep cuts and first pressings. You lose sleep thinking of obscure one-offs like Slayer's recently released "Praying to Satan: Paris Broadcast 1991" or the Pixies' "In Heaven: Live At The Emerson College 1987 – FM Broadcast." If you find yourself in a record store filled with your musical leanings, you turn into a fiend, combing the bins, racks and every square inch of the space for more hot wax and other physical format goodies.

It's the thrill of the hunt more than anything, especially for metal fans. Metal music hasn't always been widely available, though I did buy the new Killswitch Engage and Slipknot CDs at Target, and Walmart sells Motley Crue and Metallica vinyl, which is weird, but those bands have become mainstream and pop culture brands by now.

When I bought the Killswitch and Slipknot records, the young cashier asked, "Oh, what are these? DVDs?" I died a little.

The heyday of tape trading and fanzines is about as far in the past as 8-tracks. CDs have apparently joined them.

But for me there's still nothing quite like looking through crates of used records. You harbor the hope that every album you accidentally thumb past is the one you've been pining for, like a first pressing of the Stooges' self-titled 1969 release. My proudest vinyl trophy to date is an original pressing of the Misfits' "Legacy of Brutality" (1985) — the album that introduced me to a whole new world of weird music as a fourth-grader, thanks to Glenn Danzig's "Evil Elvis" vocals and Doyle's distorted rockabilly riffs from the grave.

One of my earliest, and best, friends Dylan brought the CD into class one day. He borrowed it from his older brother without telling him. At recess, all we could do was stare at the cover with its Crimson Ghost silhouette and font dripping with blood since we didn't have a CD player. Dylan raved about the songs contained within like the devil himself wrote every note. He rattled off song names that made me nervous — "Some Kinda Hate," "Angelfuck," which he whispered in my ear and we both giggled, and "Where Eagles Dare" — but I couldn't help but be intrigued. He let me take it home for a night if I promised to bring it back the next day. I must have played it 50 times that one night. I became temporarily obsessed with fully understanding and digesting Danzig's words and tone. The Misfits were a perfect gateway band for a child with a head full of Halloween haunts. Dylan risked an ass whooping for me back then, but I've been all candy apples and razorblades ever since.

The itch to find the next "Legacy of Brutality" is insatiable. The internet and social media have made searching more streamlined, but there's nothing like a boots-on-the-ground mission.

A trip to Denver isn't complete without a visit to some of the city's best record stores. When I found myself in the Mile

High City recently for a freelance gig, I made the trek to Wax Trax and Chain Reaction Records to get my fix. Wax Trax, with its mural of Lemmy (RIP) outside, is a vinyl Mecca. I always make sure to pay my respects to the madman behind Motorhead before entering.

One of the workers put on Dinosaur Jr. shortly after I arrived that particular day. "I feel the pain of everyone. Then I feel nothing."

The store's walls are covered in gig posters and promos. I spotted a Speedwolf one from an early show at the 3 Kings Tavern. The Denver-based speed metal band put out one full-length album — 2011's "Ride With Death" — that instantly became a cult classic. The metal blogs hailed it as a speed metal masterpiece at the time, as everyone in the underground waited for the band to take over the mainstream metal scene. But then they suddenly broke up and never put out another song, let alone record. "Ride With Death" — with its black-and-white cover showing a trio of werewolves riding motorcycles as the grim reaper looms large in the background — is now a metalhead measuring stick. Whenever quizzing someone about their favorite bands, the mention of Speedwolf either confirms or betrays their underground cred.

Once I saw that gig poster, I felt my pupils dilate, and my face flush. I must dig for some Denver music in the same vein, I thought. After some searching in a bin labeled "local music," I came across Weaponizer's "Lawless Age" (2017).

They had me at the promo blurb: "While one can recognize a variety of metallic sub-genre tags in the band's sound from raw black metal to post-apocalyptic thrash to Aussie war-metal to anarchic crossover, it's all menacingly welded menacingly into an indestructible shining alloy of slashing American steel." Sold!

I came down from my high, but still had an edge, so I picked up "Songs of the Plains" (2018) and "Imaginary Appalachia" (2015) by new wave outlaw country crooner Colter Wall, too. Total damage: $60. Not terrible.

I really fell off the wagon at Chain Reaction. The small, nondescript store off of Colfax is dingy and disorganized, and I love it. The shop has a stage, complete with house drum set, which feels like you're hanging out in your hesher friend's basement bedroom as they play Metallica for you for the first time.

I went straight to the used bin, where I could barely contain my excitement. At one point, I caught myself salivating and quickly wiped my mouth. No one seemed to notice.

Record after record, I pulled: Destruction's "Infernal Overkill" (1985) and "Sentence of Death" (1985, Metal Blade Records release); Noise Records' "Death Metal" sampler (1984), featuring Hellhammer, Running Wild, Helloween and Dark Avenger, with censored cover sleeve; Sodom's "The Saw Is the Law" (1991); and Combat Records' "Combat Boot Camp" EP for NYC thrashers Napalm (1986). Not to mention the seemingly countless other records I left behind. Next time, I told myself, don't want to overdo it.

On my way to the checkout counter, I picked up Haunt's "Mind Freeze" (2020) on CD and a ghoulish looking tape by a band named Nefarious (it turned out to be the four-song demo of a now-defunct death metal band from Joliet, Illinois).

An overweight Mexican man with a septum ring and a tattoo across his knuckles that said "cats rule" tallied up my haul: $158. My stomach sank a little, but then I thought if I'm ever strapped for cash, I'll sell some semen. At least my body makes more sperm, almost too much of it sometimes, but who knows when I'll come across another first pressing of Destruction's seminal "Infernal Overkill," which is German thrash glory.

"You agonize in a pool of blood

You scream out and beg for mercy
Don't try to escape or resist
'Cause Christ won't help you tonight"

Sorry, future children, but daddy's gotta get his fix.

My most recent bender cost me a total of $218. It could have been worse. It can always be worse. Plus, in Telluride, $218 buys a party animal a bag of blow and bar tab, with tip, on a typical Friday night. At least records are harder to crush up and snort.

The irony of my wax addiction is that I still need to buy a proper record player. Unfortunately, some things were left behind when I moved West, but it's time for a new rig.

A friend of a friend who visited town recently gave me some pointers on finding the right turntable.

"Spend $200 or so on a good table. None of that combo shit. And all that Crosley shit is crap."

He's a sound tech at First Avenue in Minneapolis, which is famous for being the early stomping grounds of acts like Prince, The Replacements and Husker Du. I didn't have the heart to tell him I've been eyeing a Crosley 1975T Entertainment System.

I did recently buy a Studebaker cassette player. One late night I threw on a Judas Priest "Screaming for Vengeance" tape I found many moons ago at a thrift store in western Pennsylvania. The label is hand-written, and the titles on the tape itself are almost worn away. I liked the aesthetic more than anything. The sound quality is terrible, as if Rob Halford is singing underwater, but daydreams of a fellow addict buying the tape brand new and playing it ragged filled my head.

"We are screaming for vengeance. The world is a manacled place. Screaming, screaming for vengeance. The world is defiled in disgrace."

WALK WITH ME IN HELL

I have nothing to say. As I sit here pondering a blank page, no engaging or original quips strike me. What is there to say about nothing other than it can be comforting at times, or crippling. Professionals call it writer's block — the clinical term to describe the nothingness that creeps into the brain more often than not. Symptoms include mindlessly fiddling around on other menial tasks in an attempt to ignore the blank page, self-doubt, feelings of worthlessness, the urge to run into the woods and never return, nausea, heartburn, diarrhea, and in some extreme cases, thoughts of suicide. I've experienced it so many times before that I know none of the symptoms are serious enough to be terminal, but for the rookie scribe, writer's block can be enough for them to find another profession. Those are the lucky ones. The ones with more useful skills like cleaning windows or licking envelopes for invalids.

Hitting any type of word count seems insurmountable during such droughts. I'd rather run a marathon in high heels right now. My weak ankles would surely give out and snap. The injury would require weeks of physical therapy, and I wouldn't have the time to think about anything writing related. It feels like I'm learning how to walk again at the moment anyway.

Thanks to the internet, I'm googling writing prompts in a last-ditch effort to kick start my creative juices, or whatever's left of them. The deadline approaches like death. I'm kicking myself. Real writers don't freakin' google how to write. It's supposed to just happen, as if the language lords throw down lightning bolts at worthy scribes. They must not have chosen me today. I shake my fist at the heavens, but only fools shout at the clouds and expect a response. I'm starting to seriously doubt my ability to form sentences in a somewhat pleasurable, digestible way. Sorry, valued readers, it's over. The gig is up. Bon voyage. My time to eat a bullet has come. Oh, well, it's been a good run.

But then I turn to my coworker and associate editor Suzanne Cheavens, who's also a poet and master of the written word, and explain my problem.

"Well, what does your muse look like?" she asks.

"Good question. I never really thought about it."

"Mine's a dude. ... It's basically Keith Richards."

"Mine's like a nebulous blob, I guess, like the Holy Spirit. Just out there in the ether."

Then I start to think about it more. My muse is anything and everything — the human experience, existence. The exhilaration of an adrenaline rush after conquering something you didn't think you could do. How love and lust always ignite a fire in the loins, whether you're expecting it or not. The physical pain of a broken heart and how it miraculously heals itself over time. The camaraderie of a life-long friendship. The doldrums of loss. Processing the finality of death.

I think of Charles Bukowski's poem "the crunch," published in his 1977 collection "Love Is a Dog from Hell." It ends:

who put this brain inside of me?

it cries
it demands
it says that there is a chance.
it will not say
"no."

Self-medicating with reading and music is one way I try to conjure the muse. I sit here with headphones on, about 400 words from hitting an acceptable word count. I drain out the world. The snowplow scraping past my window annoyingly beeps as it backs up and pulverizes ice and asphalt. The bumping of the bass from the early morning spin class happening in the gym below the office makes my feet tingle. The unsolicited phone calls and text messages don't stop. Everything can wait as I get into my groove.

I have my playlist on shuffle. "With A Thousand Words To Say But One" by Darkest Hour blasts into my ears.

"If we can make it through the landslide standing
We'll lift each other up to see the bliss on the horizon
Been looking in from the outside lately
I've seen who I used to be, and it's not me"

The universe is mocking my plight. I hit next.

Then it's Meshuggah's "Bleed."

"Beams of fire sweep through my head
Thrusts of pain increasingly engaged
Sensory receptors succumb
I'm no one now, only agony
My crimson liquid so frantically spilled
The ruby fluid of life unleashed"

Don't overthink it. It's been said by many word wranglers that writing is quite simple, all one must do is sit down, open up a vein and bleed onto the page.

I'm coming back to life. My brain won't say no. I'm starting to feel normal again. Maybe I just needed to drink more water and eat that banana I brought for breakfast.

Massacre's 1991 album "From Beyond," one of my favorite death metal works of all time, kicks in. The record and its cover art are homage to H.P. Lovecraft's short horror story of the same name. In it the unnamed narrator outlines his dealings with a mad scientist who invented a device that targets people's pineal glands so they can see planes of existence beyond the bounds of their accepted reality. Mayhem and carnage ensue. Monsters beyond description emerge. Reality is terrifying. I chuckle. That's exactly what having nothing to say feels like. You have to fight off the beasts that live between the ears and dig a little deeper. You can't say no.

I gave myself two hours to finish this particular piece. I have 30 minutes left. The Massacre album ends. "Flesh and the Power It Holds" by Death starts.

"It will take you in
It will spit you out
Behold the flesh
And the power it holds
Passion is a poison
Laced with pleasure bitter-sweet
One of many faces
That hide deep beneath"

I think of an ex-lover. Suddenly I'm overwhelmed with a wave of embarrassment that a younger, more romantic version of myself mistook such lust for love. I'll remember the sex forever, though. It's a fact of life I've learned to accept. Once you've become entangled with someone long enough, it's impossible not to walk away without some sort of permanent stain. She's long gone, but I still keep the husk of her memory locked up in the back of my mind to feed on sometimes. What weird webs we weave. Who put this brain inside of me? But sins of the flesh aren't so appealing anymore.

Ten more minutes and I'm ridding myself of this writing nonsense. I should have become an accountant. At least numbers are definitive. The value of words is trickier to calculate. I sit and think. Six more minutes. My emails are piling up, and I've received three more text messages. Answering them is a chore I don't want to get to anytime soon. Maybe I'll stay in purgatory a little longer. They'll understand, or maybe not. It's not something many people can relate to.

It's noon the day of deadline. There's a conspiracy of ravens gathered on the road where the snowplow cleared. I count 20 of them. There must be something edible down there. An SUV turns onto the street, and the black birds flee. The muse is gone again, but thanks for stopping by. Lamb of God's Randy Blythe is screaming at me now.

"Take hold of my hand, for you are no longer alone. Walk with me in hell."

QUARANTINED

As I write this, it's been 10 days since I've left the security of my tomb-of-a-condo and felt nature's breath. My hair is growing wildly over my ears and curling at the nape of my neck. My beard is even more unruly, as I'm seemingly reverting back to the ugly Homo sapiens I am — more of a caveman-like creature with terrible posture and a unibrow, though the gift of speech and opposable thumbs still remains. But instead of plucking edible plants from the ground or clubbing my next meal to death, I have a freezer full of microwavable Lean Cuisine meals and pizzas.

Walking my trash to the garage has become an exciting adventure of sorts that I consider "travel" at this time. I imagine anything can happen between the short distance from my front door to the dumpster. A horde of vampiric monsters could chase me down and suck me dry during this apocalyptic dawn. Then who would throw out my pizza boxes and toenail clippings. "I Am Legend" monsters aside, I'm trying to dissociate with the fact that it's me who is becoming the resident sun-shy bloodsucker who lurks in the shadows during the day only to brave the outdoors post-dusk, when I pray that most of humanity is quietly resting in their dwellings and not actively spreading the virus that's currently plaguing the world.

The overnight security guard must scratch his head whenever grainy images of a hobbling hominid flash across the still screen. He's not equipped to take down such a beast. The boss only gave him a walkie talkie to call local authorities if something serious happens and a can of pepper spray the size of a Chapstick tube, so instead of mounting any type of an attack, he holds his breath and hopes the midnight monster is a figment of his bored and tired mind. He waits for the cryptid to carry out its nightly ritual, as it always does, before scampering back to wherever it slumbers. My only hope is that I'm not causing any personal problems at home for the night guard.

But this is what we must do, I'd tell him. The government doesn't ask us to stay home and essentially do nothing for the greater good of humanity often, so I don't want to mess it up, even if it means becoming a monster.

It is nice to finally know the term for what I've been practicing for most of my adult life. Social distancing isn't just an effective way to combat the virus, according to top health officials, but also my new excuse for not hanging out with anyone after all of this passes. At least I won't have to make up bold-faced lies like I twisted my ankle getting off the pot or I'm spending time with a lady friend anymore.

Essentially every aspect of our everyday lives has been affected. It's weird to see a Burger King commercial about best "minimum contact" practices. "Let us take care of you as you take care of yourself," is the fast-food chain's new motto. Never mind a Whopper is 677 calories, including 37 grams of saturated fat (56 percent of the recommended daily intake of such poison) and 87 mg of cholesterol (29 percent). Thankfully, the closest Burger King, or any fast food, is 66 miles away in Montrose, which might as well be the Moon.

Speaking of intergalactic travel, my parents, who are both in their late 50s, are back in Pittsburgh. Dad's still working; Mum isn't. I love them, but they're stubborn. My sister and I have been hounding them about not going out in public for anything other than "essentials." They informed us Easter ham and spark plugs for the motorcycle are essential. They're getting better.

If anything happens to them, devil be damned, I imagine a chaotic scenario where I drop everything and hop into my car and drive across the country like Mad Max, fending off all the derelicts and degenerates who look like Joe Exotic along the way. I'd arrive back home a road hardened, post-apocalyptic warrior with skulls dangling from my belt and dried blood smeared under my eyes. A primal byproduct of these strange and terrible times.

In reality, however, I'm taking this time to catch up on reading, with a goal to finish at least one book a week. I also started an "extinction journal" to document all of this. Maybe the future aliens will find it useful.

I stopped watching the White House virus debriefings and reading the headlines of the national papers. The growing number of cases, both in the U.S. and across the globe, paint a dire picture that I can no longer look at and make sense of. The rising whispers of people buried in denial who believe it all to be a hoax or a politically charged ploy make me equally anxious. It seems we're suffering two viruses given such ignorance.

To dampen the reality of the situation, I started listening to black metal before noon, and enjoying a cup of black coffee and a bowl of bud before bed.

My place, which is under 1,000 square feet, has never been cleaner either. I even wipe down the baseboards now. I'm also a pro at washing dishes, like, every day. The hum of the machine is almost like the white noise of public side conversations, but better. At least the dishwasher won't try to talk to me.

Fortunately, I am still working, which is probably saving me from pure, eye-gouging insanity. Covering the pandemic can be a lot, but it's necessary and crucial, at least that's what I keep telling myself because I now fantasize about quitting on the spot and running wild into the uncertain future in doing whatever I want whenever I want, but I've always had the strength to quell that urge. It just takes me a little longer to fight it off now.

Back to the present, it's noon the day of deadline. Let's wrap this up and get on with it. I scroll Instagram briefly. A post from the British daily The Guardian pops up.

"The horror films got it wrong. This virus has turned us into caring neighbours," writes journalist George Monbiot.

The whole ordeal is oddly inspiring, I admit. Seemingly everyone is lending a helping hand — yes, even Burger King. John Krasinski's new weekly web show, "Some Good News," has become a highlight of my days indoors, if not a reason for me to openly weep, with his stories of random acts of kindness and once-in-a-lifetime connections made possible by his celebrity social circle and the immediate communication of the internet.

But my bloodshot eyes remind me that there is still work to be done. Someone has to cover the end of the world.

FACE-MELTING FURY

Warning: This piece was written
under pressure and extreme noise terror.

If wielded correctly, you can melt someone's face with an axe. It's no secret. It doesn't need to be forged from the Ark of the Covenant either. It happens all the time, every day, and people love it.

Since Robert Johnson sold his soul to the devil down in the Mississippi Delta shortly before War World II, people have been in the face-melting business. Lightnin' Hopkins, Howlin' Wolf and Muddy Waters, along with a long list of blues elder statesmen, laid the foundation by making their respective axes moan and wail with the help of electricity. Audiences responded in kind, as they helplessly became faceless fans of the tones such axemen could invoke.

Then Jimi Hendrix started fornicating with his Fender Stratocaster axe in public, before setting it on fire in an aural onstage orgy at Monterey International Pop Festival in June 1967. Hendrix's craze came after The Who's Pete Townshend smashed his axe into a stack of Marshall amps. It lives on as one of the most infamous face-melting incidents in history.

Jimmy Page had a double-necked Gibson SG axe, and sometimes he'd use a violin bow to tickle the strings. Kerry King and Jeff Hanneman seemingly tortured their down-tuned axes in creating their desired effect — solos comprised of hellish squeals reigning over chugging, chainsaw leads. Clearly, there is more than one way to be an axe murderer. If you're still skeptical, watch any of the "The Slumber Party Massacre" movies, which feature much more than just face-melting mayhem.

Having your face melted feels great, especially during live shows. Your jaw goes slack. Your eyes widen. You forget to breathe properly. Your heartbeat quickens. Sometimes a guttural "Yeah!" is accompanied by throwing up the horns. In my case, the white man's overbite and headbanging typically follow. There's something about a shredding guitar that tickles that primordial itch for satisfying vibrations. Solos. Triplets. The Devil's Tritone. Give it all to me.

While cooped up in my basement dwelling, frantically pushing out papers and riding out the cresting wave of a global pandemic, I've become more acquainted with my own axes, though I don't consider myself an axe murderer quite yet. Oh, sweet serenaders, how I've neglected you. My Ibanez acoustic accompanied me during my move West, so I've always plucked away on that, but I recently received my electric axe and amp.

It's kind of like riding a bike, though my adult brain, in memorizing more practical bits of info like proper personal finance practices, has forgotten some hard-earned guitar knowledge. Relearning the solos of Queen, Metallica and The Scorpions are on my quarantine to-do list. But I can barely read guitar tabs now, let alone sheet music, so I'll have to rely on my ears. I grabbed "100 Classic Blues Guitar Licks" and Slayer tab books to help.

The good people of Telluride Music Company are currently looking over an old DigiTech death metal pedal that makes my blues-oriented setup of a 1998 Fender Stratocaster and Hughes & Kettner amp sound like razorblades in a blender. Oh, am I ever craving that killer crunch. There's a certain level of emotion that accompanies plugging in and thrashing through Slayer's "Raining Blood."

When I first heard the now-legendary intro sometime during my adolescent years, particularly when those galloping triplets came pummeling through the speakers, my face slid down my skull and into my lap. This isn't good, I thought. It's just not right.

Growing up Catholic in a conservative corner of western Pennsylvania, Slayer scared me into believing that music had the insidious power to possess listeners in all the wrong ways, but little did I know that such a possession was exactly what I craved. I couldn't get enough.

Slayer is no longer with us. The band retired in 2018, shortly after the death of founding guitarist Jeff Hanneman. I managed to see three shows during the farewell tour, including one at Fiddler's Green in Denver.

A group of friends and I found a spot at the top of the lawn area. We partied through the sets of Napalm Death, Anthrax, Testament and Lamb of God. When Slayer finally took the stage, with Exodus axeman Gary Holt playing in place of Hanneman, the party stopped, and the sold-out crowd collectively focused its gaze on the stage. They blasted through a set filled with classics like "War Ensemble," "Dead Skin Mask" and "Angel of Death."

But when the guitars went silent and the sound of thunder broke the quiet, the crowd roared. In the distance, a real-life storm brewed behind the outdoor show. Dark clouds flashed with lightning as Slayer performed "Raining Blood" in front of the oncoming natural disaster, but the band didn't care. If anything, they seemed to be daring the gods to do something. Frontman and bassist Tom Araya screamed:

"Raining blood
From a lacerated sky
Bleeding its horror
Creating my structure
Now I shall reign in blood"

The lightning crept closer with every strike. The audience awaited its impending death. I fully expected the clouds to vomit blood onto us. We'd become a mass of skull-faced maniacs reveling in the end of everything. My friends and I high-fived in shouting, "Hell yeah!" in disbelief of the unrivaled scene. The song ended, the clouds burst, and no one was the same. The thunderstorm's rains drenched us during the closing act of the pagan baptism ritual, but instead of invoking the Apocalypse, everyone walked to their cars and drove off into the soggy night.

Simply put, Slayer is the soundtrack of the underworld. It's kind of their thing. If the elevator goes south after I expire, I fully expect to hear "Raining Blood" on my way down.

After all the 2020 festivals and concerts I planned to attend were canceled, I started pondering about melting my own face — a practice that could have serious repercussions, least among them being permanent disfigurement. Down in my dungeon I seethe. I play until my fingers are raw and my forearm cramps. My face distorts but doesn't melt. I pore over the pages of tabs in efforts to bend certain notes the right way. My right hand is more coordinated than my left. As Lemmy, an all-time face-melter on bass, once said, the left hand makes the shapes, the right hand brings them to life. Abstract analogies don't really help, but they're soothing.

Whether it's music videos, documentaries or concerts, I always look at the guitar players' hands. In the recently released ZZ Top documentary "That Little Ol' Band from Texas," seeing Billy Gibbons play up close is a revelation. He's so smooth and confident. It's like he's out there buttering bread.

Similar to writing, it's all about repetition, including listening to as much music as possible. I need music playing in the background while I write, so I treat the process like I'm studying for a double major. Subconsciously, the guitar tones and notes settle into some part of my brain only to resurface when I'm diddling away. *Wait a minute that sounds like Amon Amarth. Cue "Guardians of Asgaard." Well, hell, that's it.* Then it's time to experiment a little, changing up the rhythm and twisting it to sound fundamentally different than the original version. There's satisfaction in this, but it doesn't necessarily lead to the results I'm looking for.

Without writing a half-baked thesis, this whole face-melting phenomenon is a bit of a conundrum. I'm starting to think it's better when someone else takes their axe to your ears. Maybe it's that sense of mystery that loosens the skin around the eyes and cheeks. How did they do that? What tuning are they using? Is that a pedal or some other ungodly effect? Wait for it!

My axes rest in the corner of my living room (I never put them in their cases). I pick them up whenever I'm pacing around wondering what to work on next. Throughout the process of writing this piece, which was undertaken during an uninterrupted stretch of insanity, I picked up my Strat at least a dozen times to blast off a quick tune. A Black Sabbath riff here, and a Mayhem dirge there, even a White Zombie-Slayer-Metallica medley. Motorhead's "Overkill" and Razor's "Executioner's Song" blared while I played. It's sensory overload for sure, but I embrace such auditory chaos. Then it's back to creating this drivel. There are deadlines to hit and papers to publish. Face-melting isn't productive, but it is a nice release.

A GRENADE IN
MY HEART

There's a grenade in my heart, but I didn't pull the pin. It's been three weeks since the killing of George Floyd, an African American man who died under the knee of a now-former Minneapolis police officer. The unaltered video of his death, during which he pleaded "I can't breathe" and begged for his mother, enraged the world. How can this happen? What were the other three officers thinking as their partner nonchalantly knelt on this man's neck for nearly nine minutes? Is this normal?

People understandably reacted emotionally. Demonstrations that started in the Twin Cities spread across the nation, and then the world. The "Black Lives Matter" movement has again gained momentum in the wake of the deaths of several more unarmed African Americans, particularly the ones at the hands of police. I'd be remiss not to mention the names of Breonna Taylor, an African American woman who was shot dead in her home after Louisville police officers executed a no-knock search warrant; Ahmaud Arbery, an African American man who was fatally fired upon while jogging after a white father-and-son duo mistakenly identified him as a robbery suspect in Georgia; and Rayshard Brooks, an African American man who was shot in the back by an Atlanta police officer as he fled after failing a sobriety test in a Wendy's parking lot. There are numerous more names and similar tragic incidents that have happened since this particular spate. Their names and stories would fill this space and more, as the problem seems endless. I cried as I watched my country, my home, burn. Yes, there's a grenade in my heart, but I didn't pull the pin.

My initial anger, confusion and sadness have dampened since watching Floyd's agonizing death, but it's painfully clear that such killings aren't uncommon. Floyd's demise reignited the debate surrounding America's police brutality and racism problem. This, unfortunately, is nothing new either. America has a terrible tendency to kill progress before it can blossom into anything too big. The assassinations of the Kennedy brothers, Martin Luther King Jr. and Malcolm X come to mind. Not to mention the 1921 Tulsa race massacre, when mobs of white residents virtually wiped the African American community of Greenwood off the map, ravaging the nation's wealthiest such district known as "Black Wall Street." Clearly this country isn't as welcoming to all people, especially if you're from the African American, Latinx or Indigenous communities.

Sixty years after the civil rights movement and it seems like nothing has changed, but this feels different. There's a certain energy surrounding the current movement that I'm still trying to process.

On the threshold of 30, I've never experienced anything quite like this during my brief existence. People my age were too young to fully comprehend the impact of the 9/11 attacks and fight in the war on terrorism. My most vivid memories of that day are about being brought in from recess early because "they needed to cut the grass" and looking out the window afterward to see if the teachers were telling the truth. The grass was never cut. Soon after, several classmates were unexpectedly picked up by their parents. Even 11-year-olds knew something strange happened, but I didn't know what exactly happened until my dad told me that America was "attacked" by people who didn't like us very much. I acknowledged the seriousness of his tone, and then ran back outside to play with the neighborhood kids without thinking anything more of it.

Similarly, we were barely legal when the Great Recession hit, though many of our families felt the effects. This was at the same time we were coming of age during the ongoing opioid epidemic, which meant knowing someone who died of an overdose wasn't uncommon, especially for those of us living in rural areas. The world we met growing up wore a grim reaper's hood. Those realities can do strange things to a developing brain.

We did help elect former president Barack Obama during my young adult years, which seemed like the country, our world, was finally moving in the right direction, but then the pendulum swung as the decade ended. And the start of the new one, so far, may be one of the most tumultuous of our lifetimes, at least since we've become contributing members of society with some level of influence. Paired with the pressures and uncertainty of the COVID-19 pandemic, including economic downturn and near-record unemployment, there's even more animosity than usual.

America was founded on revolution. We learned about it in our history books. How the feisty colonials fought back against their British oppressors to create "the land of the free." But this revolution is being recorded. The connectivity of social media allows people to instantaneously share unedited videos to everyone in the world from wherever they are. Violence is always unsettling, but it's our ugly reality right now. There's a crude saying, "From shit comes flowers." Well, we have a big pile of it right now.

Like most of us, music helps me cope. I've been listening to the blues lately, as my disposition dictates. If you don't like the blues, originally played by oppressed African Americans, then how can you enjoy rock and all the many subgenres that have splintered from it? Robert Johnson's "Hellhound on My Trail" hits different right now.

"And the days keeps on worryin' me
There's a hellhound on my trail, hellhound on my trail"
Same with Albert King's "Born Under a Bad Sign."
"I can't read, haven't learned how to write
My whole life has been one big fight
Born under a bad sign
I been down since I began to crawl
If it wasn't for bad luck, I said, I wouldn't have no luck at all"
Old school hip-hop has that same down-trodden, pissed off attitude. N.W.A, Public Enemy, KRS-One, Tupac. Like the meme going around the interwebs says, "No one ever made a song called 'Fuck the Fire Department'" in reference to N.W.A's 1988 anthem "Fuck Tha Police." More recently, Kendrick Lamar has picked up the mantle, making history in 2018 for winning a Pulitzer for his "DAMN." album. But the perfect soundtrack during this current social clime is "RTJ4" by Atlanta's Run The Jewels, which is El-P and Killer Mike. Killer Mike, who is also an activist, has always been vocal about racial injustices, and the new album is brilliant. The song "JU$T," featuring Pharrell Williams and Rage Against the Machine's Zack de la Rocha, has one of the cleverest choruses I've ever heard — *"Look at all these slave masters posin' on yo' dollar."*

But "pulling the pin" gives me goosebumps. With guest vocals by Mavis Staples, as well as guitar work by Josh Homme (Ex-Kyuss, Queens of the Stone Age, Eagles of Death Metal), she croons, *"There's a grenade in my heart and the pin is in their palm."*

DEATH & DOOM AT DIA

F lying on a plane during the COVID-19 pandemic is terrifying, let alone idiotic, according to smart people. In a popular New York Times survey, only 7 percent of the 511 epidemiologists polled admitted that they would travel by air during such a public health disaster.

But I've never claimed to be smart, so I took my chances and experienced the doom-laden dread of cramming myself into a metal bird with other possibly afflicted humans as I flew back to Pittsburgh for my best friend's wedding in June 2020. As the best man, it's an occasion I wouldn't miss for the world, even though he planned to have me there virtually and postponed the bigger ceremony to 2021. If I died en route, the blood would not be on his hands.

Arriving at the Denver International Airport around 11 p.m. for a 1:30 a.m. redeye to Charlotte, where I had a three-hour layover before heading to the Steel City, I parked about seven miles from the terminal, took a long piss next to my car, inhaled a deep breath and dove into the maelstrom.

I've been to Denver's airport dozens of times, but on this night, it seemed off-kilter. I couldn't find the American Airlines desk or a living person to ask where to go. I wandered aimlessly for what felt like an eternity. My pulse pounded inside my noise-canceling headphones to create a dirge-like drumbeat. I became lost, confused, irritated and directionless.

Once thoroughly disoriented, I decided to give in. This is purgatory. I must have fallen victim to a violent crash. Somewhere along I-70 in Glenwood Canyon, I imagined myself drifting in and out of consciousness. This airport must be my dying vision.

The south security entrance, which is the one I typically use with the large American flag hanging from the ceiling, had been closed for construction. The north security checkpoint was on the other side, under the gigantic Colorado flag, a friendly TSA employee who noticed my concern told me. But blank, white walls blocked off a large section of the walkway to the only open entrance. Again, I walked in circles. After several detours, I found the line. An attractive couple and I were the only passengers present aside from the TSA skeleton crew. Even the drug-sniffing dogs had the night off.

I asked the lady overseeing the conveyor belt if any airport establishments were open.

"McDonald's."

Of course there's fast food in the afterlife, I thought. "What about bars? I was thinking I'd get drunk before my flight." A friend who recently traveled by air suggested eating a Xanax beforehand, but another flight-weary comrade said a couple of mini-bottles of vodka would have the same effect.

"That much time, huh? No, everything closes down around 6 p.m. ... except McDonald's. You should have been here a month ago, it was like the apocalypse."

"Yeah, it feels like it. Where are the drug dogs?"

"Oh, they have a random schedule now. They're like never here anymore, especially when we're this dead."

The security guard admitted her amateur stature without even realizing it. She could have been talking to El Chapo for all she knew. Sharing such precious information about the drug detection schedule could have serious consequences, but I only wanted to get nice and drunk on this night.

But damn it all. I'd have to navigate this post-mortem labyrinth stone sober. At that time, after successfully passing through security, I decided to remove my glasses. And blind.

I found the only McDonald's south of heaven at the top of the Terminal A escalator. Ronald McDonald was getting his ass handed to him, as a gaggle of my fellow near-dead travelers piled into the four socially distanced lines, while a small herd waited off to the side for their orders to be called.

I began to sweat and panicked when I found myself in front of the cashier, "A large sweet tea and two bottles of water ... "

"Anything else?"

"Do you have any alcohol ... for the tea?"

"No."

"OK, that's it."

I typically order more at such an establishment. The feel of fast food grease in my blood is a cheap high for a glutton. The heart slows, the belly bulges, and the bowels start moving. But I couldn't risk soiling myself on this night. Liquid only.

A lady with arms that ended at her elbows handed me my receipt — Order No. 369 — through the porthole of the protective Plexiglas shield. I began to murmur the song of the same name.

"*3, 6, 9*
The goose drank wine
The monkey chewed tobacco on the streetcar line
The line broke, the monkey got choked
And they all went to heaven in a little rowboat"

Oh, sweet insanity, you cruel jokester. One cannot even get

high on the meats that made him on such a journey. I grabbed my drinks and scurried to find a spot at my gate. Landing in a seat facing the window overlooking the airport apron behind a large pillar, I tore off my facemask and quickly consumed all my drinks. A lady nearby stared in horror as dribble fell from my chin and onto my chest. I returned the glare, as if to say, "Mind your own fuckin' funeral."

As a metal and hip-hop mix played through my headphones, I sat there, blind, reading "The Collected Schizophrenias" by Esmé Weijun Wang, which is a collection of powerful essays about the author's life with mental illness, but it did nothing to assuage my anxiety on this night.

I checked my news app, "BREAKING: UFOs over Wisconsin?" Thank God, finally. Take me with you, I'd plead to the space travelers. You can probe me and make fun of my wonky human anatomy. I don't know how such a poorly built species survived this long either, but I'll show you where the men in black suits keep all the aliens imprisoned in the Nevada desert. Just get me off of this festering rock.

I began to write in my Moleskine. In checking my notes from that fearful night while preparing this piece, I can barely discern my scrawls. In no particular order:

"Ignore the other humans enjoying their McDonald's as if it's their last meal."

"If you're gonna die, die with a Big Mac in your belly."

"'The weirdo in the corner won't stop writing,' I hear them whisper. 'I'll die if I do!' I scream back."

"DIA (Denver International Airport) is eerily similar to DOA (dead on arrival)."

"If you were ever going to expose yourself in public, this would be the time."

"The lady watching you is one of them. Maybe she's your escort to nirvana."

"This really gives new meaning to 'through hell and high water.'"

But once aboard the initial flight, I passed out before we took off. It was the type of sleep that feels final — no dreams or sudden awakenings, only the infinite blackness of the brain shutting off.

I slept-walked until arriving in Pittsburgh, where a friend picked me up. We immediately headed to Primanti Brothers for oversized sandwiches and Iron City beers. I drank six.

The aliens never did come for me, but all hysterics aside, I'd gladly relive the fear-induced fever dream as Darin and Maggie were officially married in front of a small group of family and friends during a quaint ceremony in downtown Pittsburgh. Congratulations, Lyles.

THE BEAUTIFUL GAME

I t's game day in August, but I'm not getting ready to watch the NFL, which would typically be nearing the end of preseason. Neither am I all jacked up about the restart of the NHL Stanley Cup or NBA playoffs, especially after my hometown Pittsburgh Penguins failed to qualify after losing a five-game series to the worst team in the bubble-centric format, the Montreal Canadiens. Baseball? Nope. I'm talking about soccer (or futbol, to the diehards, but I'll go with the Americanized "soccer" for this piece to avoid confusion with American football). I'm writing this as Bayern Munchen and Lyon play a UEFA Champions League semifinals match. With hockey and basketball dominating the primetime sports channels, I'm watching the Spanish-speaking broadcast, so I have no idea what they're saying, but I don't necessarily need to. Ah, the beautiful game.

Like everything else, the COVID-19 pandemic halted all sports for a certain period of time. But as the human race began to cope and adapt to the new socially distanced normalcy that the coronavirus brought, soccer became the first pro sport to return — first in Europe, then stateside, with the MLS is Back Tournament, which started July 8, 2020, and took place at Florida's ESPN Wide World of Sports Complex. And I can't get enough.

Before I get all "Green Street Hooligans" here, my soccer experience and fandom up until this point is minimal at best. The height of my soccer playing "career" spanned those cherished years when Capri Suns and Dunkaroos were considered proper post-game nourishment. I don't even remember which position I played back then, but I do remember we were the Raptors because dinosaurs were cool. I had delusions of grandeur of becoming the first Jurassic soccer player in history, as I spent a good three weeks walking everywhere on my tiptoes pretending to be Reptar and making dino noises. In preparation for my big debut, I studied "The Land Before Time" because "Jurassic Park" gave me nightmares at that age.

We also had an end-of-season banquet at McDonald's where we all ate a bunch of chicken nuggies and were given trophies even though we didn't win a game. A proper Millennial childhood.

My parents like to tell a story about my days on the pitch. I must have been tasked with playing defense, or maybe they threw me in goal, but I had no clue what to do, so I ran up on the ball like a baby Beckham. The official immediately stopped the game and walked me back to my proper place, where I proceeded to sit in the grass, pick at dandelions and pout until I got a juice box. Score.

The first half just ended with tournament favorite Bayern up 2-0. I'm reviewing what I wrote and asking myself why the hell I'm musing about my childhood athletic failures, but there's no time to second guess it. The 15 minutes between halves goes fast, and the action will start again soon.

Childhood obesity forced me to trade in my soccer shoes for American football cleats, which I wore through college. But as a fan of sports and competition in general I'd always get wrapped up in the World Cup, especially Italy's 2006 championship and the United States women's national team's 2019 top finish. Pittsburgh has a team, too — the Riverhounds, now of the United Soccer League Championship — but I didn't pay much attention to them until I landed a catering job at the team's beautiful, then-new stadium on the city's South Side. The passion of the Steel Army — the team's supporter club — caught my attention more than anything. They all have so much fun making a racket and chanting.

I dove into the passionate Pittsburgh soccer scene even deeper when I picked up a freelance gig covering the city's proper English soccer pub where all the footballers hung out. Piper's Pub welcomed an eclectic mix of punk rockers and Mexican nationals, English expats and young hipsters who unironically wrapped themselves in supporter scarves. As much as pints were central to the celebration, the early morning openings to air English Premier League matches were just as raucous.

A middle-aged man named Alex, who worked at the pub and served as the unofficial spokesman for the group of pick-up players I was writing about, talked about the small knit community soccer created within the city. Teams featured people of all backgrounds from longtime locals like Alex to Latin Americans who recently moved to Pittsburgh.

They'd find a field, typically on the city's North Side, and play for hours. The games were inherently meaningless, but that wasn't the point. The game creates a universal language.

During a high school trip to Ocean City, Maryland, my friends and I met a group of guys our age from Nepal that played soccer on the sand each night in front of our boardwalk hotel.

We jumped in one night, and when it became too dark to play on the beach, we all played under the dim lights of the hotel and nearby storefronts into the early morning. At the same time every night, we met up and played boardwalk soccer. The risk of splinters and stubbed toes didn't matter. When the ball our Nepalese friends brought busted, our games ceased. But we were determined to keep the nightly meetups going, so my friends and I went out and bought them a new one as a "thank you" gift for sharing the beautiful game with us. We brought it to their place, which was a short walk from where we were staying, and they cooked us an impromptu dinner of chicken curry and ran out to buy beer. We didn't expect food and drinks, but they explained that was customary in their culture whenever guests came to the house. We didn't play soccer that night, but it remains one of my favorite soccer memories.

After that, and the magazine feature, I had a newfound appreciation for watching the beautiful game. The endless motion. The skill. The nuance. The stamina. The crowd's contagious energy in displaying such rabid civic pride.

Watching the MLS and Premier League matches recently made me a full-fledged soccer fan. I decided to throw my support behind the Wolverhampton Wanderers, also known as Wolves, which happens to be Robert Plant's hometown club. I've even subscribed to the Birmingham (England) Mail's daily Wolves email updates. The Wanderers were knocked out of the UEFA tournament by juggernaut Sevilla during the quarterfinals, 1-0, though the boys from England's West Midlands gave the Spaniards a scare. The pesky play of Wolves had me on the edge of my seat for 90-plus minutes. I can't wait for the club's 2020-21 Premier League fixtures to be announced. The new season is set to kick off next month.

For now, I'm sitting by myself watching Bayern dominate play. The Bavarian side scored a third goal, and the Spanish-speaking broadcasters went wild. Soccer celebrations are comically over the top, but if I had to run 10-plus miles a match I'd probably take my shirt off and hug everyone in sight, too, whenever I found the back of the net.

After three minutes of stoppage time, Bayern takes it 3-0. It's the last semifinal match. The upcoming Sunday final will feature Paris Saint-Germain and Bayern. One more beautiful game.

MY LITTLE CYCLOPS

I'm not one to be too sappy, especially publicly, but this is a love letter I must share with everyone. On the eve of Halloween, I've recently fallen for a Cyclops, and it's going great so far. It's not as interesting as you may think, though the unusual union happened suddenly. While proof-reading the paper one afternoon, I couldn't help but notice an ad for a one-eyed black kitten named Ripley.

The mugshot of the four-month-old misfit couldn't have been rougher. He looked like he'd been on the losing end of a street fight with a switchblade. The socket of his recently removed eye had been glued shut, and his ruffled fur gave him a disheveled appearance. The description explained how Ripley made lemonade out of the lemons life handed him. He was perfect.

I immediately called the humane society and submitted my adoption application. I've always wanted a small army of black cats, but never met the right one. At that moment, Ripley and I seemed destined to be together.

The next day I found myself at the store perusing the pet aisle for everything I'd need for my little Cyclops — kitten chow, litter box, toys — before heading to Ripley's house, where I decided to go through with the adoption, even though he didn't pay much attention to me. He's playing it cool, I thought, but I was nervous he didn't like me.

The people at the humane society told me Ripley's mother and litter were recently rescued from a hoarding situation. Mom and his siblings found forever homes quickly, but Ripley remained.

He'd lost his left eye after his cornea ruptured due to an upper respiratory infection he suffered from living in such filth. They also fixed him when they operated on the eye. To say he had a rough couple of weeks would be an understatement. But other than that, he was a healthy kitten.

Some may see his ocular oddity as grotesque. What hellish world claims a kitty's eye, you might wonder. I'd say it's quite the opposite. Cyclopes can see the future, as they made a deal with Hades that cost them one of their eyes, leaving them with only one in the center of their foreheads, according to Greek mythology. Hesiod's Cyclopes were also the blacksmiths of the gods, crafting thunderbolts for Zeus, an invisibility helmet for Hades and Poseidon's trident.

In the month since my little Cyclops moved to Telluride, he hasn't spent much time hovering over a hearth or prophesizing like some one-eyed Nostradamus, but he does have special powers, I've discovered.

Whenever I lie down to read or rest, Ripley jumps onto my chest, and we lay face to face. As he purrs and plays with my beard, he'll nudge his head forward, and we'll rub our noses together. I call this display of affection a Ripley kiss, and it's one of the purest forms of love I've experienced, even when he wakes me up at 4 a.m. to give me one.

While I spend most of my days hunched in front of the work computer, Ripley sits next to me, rubs against my feet or rolls around the coffee table in front of the screen, particularly when I'm not giving him enough attention. One busy workday I threw one of his mouse toys across the room. He quickly ran after it, and within seconds, brought it back to my feet. Between editing and writing, I'd toss the mouse to different areas, and every time, Ripley brought it back to me. If I didn't grab and throw it quickly enough for him, he'd meow and bite my big toe. I can't believe it, I said to myself, he taught me how to play fetch. Now he knows to drop a toy on my toes whenever he wants to burn some kitty calories.

When I'm not on the clock, Ripley and I like to watch TV to relax. He enjoys sports, especially baseball and football. It's funny to watch him follow the action so attentively, head bopping, ears twitching. When we're watching the Steelers on Sunday I like to say he's a black-and-gold cat.

Halloween season also means horror movies, and Ripley is coming around. He's not immune to jump scares, though, so he prefers the black-and-white classics. We recently watched "Cat People." He seemed to like Simone Simon's shape-shifting character.

My Aunt Debbie, an avid animal lover and activist, told me I'll start hating people now that I own a kitty. That's already the case, I explained. We both laughed and continued to talk about the benefits of cats. But don't take our word for it. For as much as he wrote about hangovers and hookers, Charles Bukowski can be viewed as a pseudo cat expert or oracle. He once linked our furry friends to immortality.

"The more cats you have, the longer you live. If you have a hundred cats, you'll live ten times longer than if you have ten. Someday this will be discovered, and people will have a thousand cats and live forever."

Maybe people with a legion of cats aren't "crazy" after all.

There's a whole book of Bukowski's cat musings.

Like this, "Having a bunch of cats around is good. If you're feeling bad, just look at the cats, you'll feel better, because they know that everything is, just as it is."

My little Cyclops blinks his phantom eye as I chuckle to myself over such quotes. To think, some people believe black cats are bad luck. It's a uniquely Western myth, as black cats are considered good luck in Japanese culture. Ironically, the Greeks are the ones responsible for casting felines with black fur in such an unfavorable light.

During the time of gods and monsters, Hera, Zeus' wife, turned her servant Galinthias into a black cat as punishment after she tried to hinder the birth of Hercules. Galinthias then went to work for Hecate, the goddess of witchcraft, and black cats have gotten a bad rap ever since.

I look at Ripley and smile. That's funny, I tell him, in my experience, it's the blondes with their two big blue eyes that have always been the harbingers of horror and hardship.

Fun fact: A previous version of this story won a Best of Writing-Nonfiction contest organized by Western Colorado University's Pathfinder magazine.

BARBERSHOP BANTER

As I've explained, personal appearance hasn't been my highest priority during the pandemic. Since my coworkers and I have been working from home, I only see them once a week via Zoom, even then it's only from the neck up.

Combing my hair and throwing on a hat is dressing up nowadays, as sweatpants, graphic tees and cat hair have been my main wardrobe around the house.

Hair doesn't stop growing though, so I recently found myself in need of a good trimming after four months of no maintenance.

Without a proper barbershop in town, I traveled many miles to find a chair. When I walked in to the Montrose business, I saw there were three other guys, not including the two currently getting a cut. After exchanging pleasantries — the customary guy greeting of a head nod and "How you doing?" — I took my seat at the end of the worn-out leather bench and waited.

Socially distancing in the small space was impossible, but no one seemed to care anyway. I had a facemask on me, but I didn't put it on in fear of ridicule or death. Adopting the herd mentality in this instance was necessary.

A burley man with a shaved head and long Viking beard held court. His shirt looked two sizes too small, especially around his meaty biceps, and he swore like a sailor. He talked about a successful raid he recently led.

"We tracked this fucker down to Trinidad, then six of us jumped out of this van with ARs (semi-automatic rifles)," he gloated. "He about shit himself, like 'What's going on?'"

The other gentlemen in the barbershop snickered and asked questions.

"How many days were you down there?"

"Two days. It took us only two days to find this fuckin' guy. He was an idiot, posting on social media and shit like a fuckin' moron," the modern-day Mongol said.

"What was he wanted for?"

"A buncha things," the brute said without specifying if he had hunted down a high-profile serial killer or petty pot dealer. "He had a $1 million bond, so we were like, 'Fuck yeah we'll head down there.' Got into the million dollar club with that one."

He never did describe who "we" were, but I surmised that this man, who had his toddler son with him, had to be some kind of Dog the Bounty Hunter type who got his kicks by cracking skulls and pillaging. I decided not to engage in the conversation because I didn't want him to club me over the head like a baby seal and scalp me for fun, but I noticed he kept glancing in my direction.

Jesus Christ, this madman is a bloodthirsty savage. He's going to punch a hole through my face and feed me to his barbershop buddies. What did I walk into? My vanity will be my demise.

The brute spoke to me, "Garrett?"

"What?"

"You're Garrett."

"No. Justin."

He laughed a little, "I'm sorry. You look exactly like this guy Garrett I know."

One of the barbers who also sported a bald dome and long beard joked that he thought I was a criminal on the lam.

"I figured you knew him from one of your mugshots," he said.

"Do I look that bad?"

"No, no," the Viking said. "I just thought you were someone else."

He asked me what I do and where I'm from. I lied. Head-hunters like that don't need much to track you down. Lord knows I don't need a hitman haunting me with the head full of ghosts I already harbor.

"I sell Polaroid pictures of my feet online."

Everyone laughed. An older man with salt-and-pepper hair and sad, watery eyes coughed up phlegm, then spoke, "I just come here to hangout."

Everyone nodded their heads in agreement.

"I just like having a stranger hold a straight razor to my throat," I said. "Makes me feel something."

The bald owner cleaned off his chair and called me up. Images of Sweeney Todd, the Demon Barber of Fleet Street, flashed through my head, but then I imagined a slasher movie called "Nails" (working title) that features a vial of red nail polish that contains the blood of Satan. Whoever wears it becomes possessed. As my hair fell in clumps below me, I conjured up the perfect main character — a flamboyant Black drag queen. Images of RuPaul ripping out people's throats and chewing on cheeks came to mind, but then the barber chair fell backwards. I snapped back to reality. A warm towel covered my face, as the shaving ritual started.

I laid there blind and vulnerable. The bald owner explained how business has been affected by the pandemic, including a closure of several months, but now they're operating with proper guidelines in place.

"It's crazy," he said. "Sometimes we didn't know what to do."

The Viking left with his young son, who took a Halloween-sized bag of Sour Patch Kids from the shop's plastic pumpkin.

"We'll see you at the Elks tonight," he said.

After the barbarian left, the guys talked about his many tall tales of chasing criminals. He seemed just as much a character to them as he did to me. I also wasn't alone in thinking he had a flair for the dramatic.

"He talks like he's Rambo," one man said.

"He wishes," another added.

The barber whipped his razor around my neck without a second thought.

He's done this countless times, and to my knowledge, hasn't killed anyone. A fresh shave is refreshing, especially with the hot towel treatment before and after.

With my skin burning, the barber rubbed some type of balm all over my face, then another towel — the final phase of my manscaping. I heard someone mention how the local high school football team is doing. They should beat their next opponent by at least 40 points.

Everyone talked as if there isn't a deadly virus shattering society as we know it.

I paid the barber and thanked him for the fresh cut. Maybe I'll wait more than four months next time.

EXTINCTION JOURNALS

In reflecting on 2020, all I can think is, shoot this dying bastard in the head, set it aflame and let's dance among the falling ashes. But the masses still can't gather in large numbers yet, due to the COVID-19 pandemic.

In March, when society crumbled under the weight of the virus, I began an "extinction" journal to chronicle the external and internal insanity of this plague-stricken year. Three Moleskines and counting later, I'm rereading my musings for this piece. Most of the writings couldn't be reprinted here due to language or descriptions of degenerate, illegal behavior, and the below excerpts were edited for exactly that.

THURSDAY, *March 19, 2020*

I don't mind too much if this is the new normal. People are being nicer and kinder to one another. Pollution has decreased, too. Maybe Mother Nature knows what's best for her and us.

Work has been crazy since Thursday, March 12, after the virus took over the nation. We're doing important work, though. These are "unprecedented times," everyone keeps saying. It's kind of exciting covering the end of the world. Strangely, I'm feeling more inspired than I have in a while. Think this is going to produce some good work. Hard to take my mind off it. Getting high and letting the mind wander helps.

For some reason, with all this talk of isolation and quarantine, all I want to do is fuck. Luckily, I have a girl to do that with. She lives in the housekeeping suite of a mansion in Mountain Village, but since no one is staying there for a while, she has the whole place to herself. So, I headed up there for some drunks and sex. She asked me to bring my Polaroid camera, too. She likes when I take nude photos of her, so I did. We drank red wine, made it a few times in the master bedroom — she's an acrobatic lay — and took a bath afterward. I bent her over the sink before we dried off.

We've talked about keeping it casual. I have no interest in anything serious right now. All I want to do is write, fuck and watch it all end.

THURSDAY, *March 26, 2020*

I'm high. Just sent my Sunday story to (Associate Editor Suzanne Cheavens) and smoked a bowl. Now I'm watching a Pink Floyd documentary. It's such a stoner thing to do, but I love Pink Floyd. Have you ever listened to "Wish You Were Here," "Dark Side of the Moon," "The Wall" or "The Division Bell?" I mean, damn. It's immortal music. It's in the bones. Damn, I dig Pink Floyd. I'll fight you to the death about their greatness. Trippy, blues-based rocked turned psychedelia. But I think you need to be stoned to fully, properly, enjoy them.

Anyway, it was a standard, or at least what's defined as standard now, day at work. Finished and made some dinner (pork chops and broccoli). Then I finished watching "Tiger King" on Netflix, before finding the Floyd doc.

What mad geniuses they all were, unlike all the creatures of "Tiger King." How lucky we are to be able to listen to and enjoy Pink Floyd. Same with Black Sabbath. All geniuses. They literally created a new sound that spawned a new musical genre — heavy metal — that spawned seemingly countless subgenres. Without Black Sabbath you don't have the New Wave of British Metal, thrash, hardcore, death metal, black metal (first and second wave), the New Wave of American Heavy Metal, grindcore, metalcore, Swedish death metal, groove metal, sludge, doom/stoner metal, nu metal and so on. It can all be traced back to Black Sabbath.

It's crazy how much of an impact they've had on alternative music and how recently it all happened. My dad is older than heavy metal. He also loves Pink Floyd and Black Sabbath, so I remember listening to both bands growing up. We both agree that Floyd's best work was the "Dark Side of the Moon" to "Animals" era of the 1970s. He even admitted he wasn't the biggest fan of "The Wall," which he called "poppy." We also both agree that the best way to listen to Pink Floyd is stoned. Give it a try if you've never done it and you'll get it. If you don't, then I truly feel sorry for you.

APRIL 1, 2020

There are six new cases in the county — seven total now. None of them are serious as all seven people self-isolated and are recovering "well," as officials put it.

Still haven't left the house. I'm used to it. Having a minigout flare up, which is always annoying. Luckily, I don't have to go anywhere. Called in a new prescription, too. My diet and exercise routine has been messed up by this shit. I'm not really exercising at all, and I'm snacking more since I'm stuck inside. Gotta change it up. It's too easy to be lazy.

Was supposed to fly to Iceland today. Obviously, that trip got canceled. It's a bummer. Karlee (my sister) and I were so excited about it, our first time in Europe. Hopefully we'll be able to do it sooner rather than later. This year seems to be a fucking loss already. Just delay everything a year basically. This pandemic is insane, but one day we'll look back and make fun of how unbelievable it all was. We can all say we lived through history. It's not that exciting.

MAY 25, 2020

Called Grandma today. Haven't talked to her in a while, so it was nice catching up. She's doing well, for the most part. She told me some of my great ancestors, including my great-great-grandmother, died during the 1918 Spanish flu pandemic after moving to Pennsylvania from Scotland. She said they're all buried in DuBois, Pennsylvania, in a cemetery she hasn't been to since she was little. Would like to go back there with her, but who knows when we'll be able to travel.

JULY 4, 2020

Fourth of July didn't feel the same. With the pandemic and general disarray of the country, I really didn't care to celebrate. Got up early and hiked up Bear Creek to the Wasatch trailhead. There was some weather, so I hiked down quickly.

SEPT. 2, 2020

The end of the world is taking longer than I expected. Humanity, particularly here in America, has had enough time to embarrass itself over and over again. ... Each century humans are doomed to repeat the errors of the past. When will the new generations learn and break the patterns of our parents?

Oct. 31, 2020

Is 2020 actually happening or did the Earth slip away from the Sun's gravitational pull and drift into the cold death of space and everyone is trapped in a cosmic coma nightmare?

ARISE

The writing process for these chronicles of chaos typically includes sifting through random anecdotes and blurbs from various times during the preceding weeks as I attempt to edit them into one coherent piece that could be printed.

This one is no different in that sense, except I couldn't ignore how January didn't magically bring new beginnings and peace on Earth in acting like the thirteenth month of 2020.

Are we stuck in a time loop? Why is everybody acting like the clock is going to save us?

Initially I thought the dawn of 2021 and a new presidency would finally silence and banish the foolishness of the past four years, particularly 2020, but the Jan. 6, 2021, insurrection of the Capitol caught me, like most people, totally off guard.

Enraged, I wrote: "The followers and fanatics of the now-former, thankfully, orange in the oval office dug in their heels and blindly stormed the Capitol to avenge the legal loss of their Cowardly Lion of a leader. There's not enough space on this page to dive into the irony and hypocrisy of it all. Our nation's political experiment seems to be boiling over the beaker, but instead of coming together to carefully clean it up, we'd rather scream and recklessly riot in its ever-flowing acidity, while hating one another more and more for being burnt by our own creation. Ah, democracy."

That evening, while still contemplating the state of the country, I put "Texas Sun" on the turntable. Ripley, my one-eyed black cat, rested on my desk chair. He doesn't know who Leon Bridges is, but I scooped him up and cradled him in my arms anyway to dance around my apartment to "Conversion."

"I was a prisoner living in my prison
Of ignorance my mouth full of curses and bitterness
I was chained to my sin I was lovin'
Evil deeds in the dark
I was huggin' them tight
Close my eyes was clouded with lust for the adulteress
But her ways lead to death
I was on my way to hell
Ridin' on a train first class"

Ripley doesn't know what hell is. I set him on the kitchen table. His rumpled long hair made him look like Church from "Pet Sematary."

How much can one person write about being alone in their condo with their cat during these cursed times?

He didn't answer. Not that I expected him to. Instead, he licked his paw and jumped to the floor. The record ended. Images of the Jan. 6 insurgence continued to play across the muted television in the living room.

New year, same problems.

The working title for this piece was "13/6/2020," but I scrapped it after I sobered up and settled down.

Quit trying to be so goddamn edgy.

The title reminded me of my acid-eating college buddy. Once when we were smoking a joint in the woods at the edge of campus he told me about a novel he started writing that centered around the annihilation of time as we know it. In the future, all clocks were stuck at 88:88 for no apparent reason. Mayhem ensued, woodland creatures wandered into big cities and, well, it didn't make much sense. Kind of like the past 13 months, but the clock seems to be blinking 20:20.

Ironically, the Earth is spinning faster than ever. According to scientists that study such things, the 28 fastest days ever recorded occurred in 2020, which is further proof that this is all made up and nothing really matters. Unfortunately, the planet won't reach speeds fast enough to disrupt its gravitational pull that's keeping everything in place anytime soon.

The government quietly released thousands of documents in 2020 that all but provide photographic evidence that aliens exist, and world leaders have known about them forever. Numerous military accounts, mainly from the United States Air Force, outline encounters with UFOs over the past several decades. The feds even divulged a grainy video taken from an aircraft video camera that details a UFO chase. The pilots are stunned to come across the fast-moving object that seemingly doesn't abide by earthly mechanics. The Black Vault, an online archive of government documents related to odd happenings like extraterrestrial life and paranormal activities, has more than 3 million documents anyone can sift through.

Why isn't this the story of the freakin' century?

Oh, right. I forgot about the threat of a global nuclear holocaust that welcomed the new decade, the fires of biblical proportions that nearly claimed an entire continent down under, the swaths of locusts that engulfed parts of Africa, toilet paper shortages, murder hornets, police brutality, the border debacle and how half of all Americans willingly joined a cult in the name of patriotism.

Plus, Kobe died. Charlie Daniels died. John Lewis died. Ruth Bader Ginsberg died. Gale Sayers died. Chadwick Boseman died. Eddie Van Halen died. Sean Connery died. Whitey Ford died. Bob Gibson died. Lou Brock died. Neil Pert died. Regis Philbin died. Little Richard died. John Prine died. Leslie West died. Floyd Little died.

That's not to mention the nearly half million Americans who have now died during the ongoing pandemic that rivals only the Black Plague.

New York City started filling up its potter's field on Hart Island with their dead; many buried in mass graves without any proper identification or marker. Los Angeles County temporarily suspended all cremations due to air quality concerns; leaving the corpses to rot in the morgue. There's a three-headed dragon flying over the heartland belching and burning all of the country's crops. There isn't, obviously, but how bad is it when a dragon is the least medieval-sounding scourge in the past year?

Recently, with all this on my mind, and while listening to "Damnation" off of Morbid Angel's 1989 death metal master-piece "Altars of Madness," I felt something like this:

"Damnation
Fill the world with plague
Force of devastation
Tyranny from above"

With a hard deadline and no more time to spin my wheels, I'm relating more to Sepultura's "Arise," from the 1991 album of the same name.

"Obscured by the sun
Apocalyptic clash

Cities fall in ruin
Why must we die?
Obliteration of mankind
Under a pale grey sky
We shall arise"

CASE OF THE MONDAYS

It's 4 a.m. when my alarm clock initially goes off. It starts with a quiet meow followed by faint footsteps along my chest and neck. Then I hear the purring. Ripley is making sure Daddy's alive. He kneads in my armpit as if he's preparing a ball of fresh dough, before settling on my left shoulder, resting his head on my cheek. I grunt and kiss him so he knows I'm not dead. Some mornings I fear Ripley will start gnawing my face off otherwise. I also take this as an opportunity to change sleeping positions and check the clock. It is still dark, but dawn is near.

I fall back asleep until 7 a.m., when Ripley again repeats his morning ritual across my belly. The day's first light fights through the nearby window blinds. I can make out his inky profile.

He's the most innocent, beautiful, perfect creature alive at that moment. If pharaohs still reigned, they'd build a 10,000-foot statue of him. It'd be bigger than the Great Sphinx of Giza, and people from around the globe would make pilgrimages to Egypt to worship the giant one-eyed idol. Oh, my immortal cat god, take pity on us humans for we are foolish in all of our pride, greed, gluttony, anger, envy, lust and laziness.

I roll out of bed around 7:30 a.m. and quickly start my morning calisthenics, which include stretching and resistance band work. Whenever I lie on the ground for sit-ups, Ripley juts underneath my legs, but I've become quick at scooping him up and holding him against my chest while I do them. I can do 30 now.

The short workout is followed by standard personal hygiene practices. While brushing my teeth, I use a silk toothbrush and charcoal whitening toothpaste, followed by thorough flossing — always the bottom row first, from left to right. I finish my oral routine by rinsing my mouth out with zero-alcohol mouthwash because zero-alcohol mouthwash has a "less intense taste," but still "kills 99.9 percent of bad breath germs," the label explains.

Once properly dressed — black gym shorts and a gray crewneck sweater that says "C.L.A.W.S. Cat Lovers Against White Supremacy" — I wake up my computer, which comes back to life with a low hum and electronic groan. While it's thinking, I turn on the TV and find ESPN. "First Take" is always on at this early hour. The show's talking heads are again debating the greatness of LeBron James. It's a tired topic, practical sports fanatics know Michael Jordan is the best athlete to ever make his living on the hardwood, but they need to fill airtime.

I briefly listen to the arguments for LeBron being the greatest of all time — I'll never be convinced — before making my way to the kitchen. I believe in a well-balanced diet, so I put together a protein shake — one scoop of vegan chocolate almond coconut flavored powder, mixed with almond milk, organic honey and organic cinnamon — and grab an organic banana for breakfast every morning.

By the time I finish my meal, emails from the last three days are fully loaded. There are 157 this morning.

I begin to tediously go through them. Most are junk and quickly deleted, but Grandmasfathack@leanbelly.net sends me a note with an intriguing subject line: "I don't want you to see me naked!"

"After menopause caused 60-year-old Karen to gain 30lbs of fat...

She felt unattractive... unloved... alone... and OLD.

The extra weight was KILLING her confidence... and literally stealing YEARS away from her life.

But Karen's near-death experience ultimately led to an unusual discovery that changed everything ...

Luckily, her doctor discovered a simple 10-sec trick that BLOCKS fat storage and allows any person over 40 to melt off ONE pound of fat cells per day...

And Karen went on to lose 22lbs directly from her menopause belly!"

Good for Karen, but decay is inevitable. I delete over half of my emails this morning, saving only the ones from real people with real questions and concerns, including a request to investigate how much dog poop actually piles up on public trails. Some are legitimate article ideas, though, which I share during our Monday editorial Zoom meeting at noon. In gathering a list of potential stories for the week ahead, I also always check my phone for a text message from George Soros. Still nothing.

Once all four editorial employees are on the Zoom call, we chat about our weekend and joke about the redundancy of pandemic life, particularly how we seemingly cover the same thing each week — the pandemic is still here, cases are still rising, it's still not wise to tongue fuck strangers in bars.

Since I haven't splurged for the upgraded Zoom package,

our story meetings are limited to 40 minutes, which is typically more than enough time for us to plan the week's four papers.

Afterwards, I focus on reaching out to sources, while simultaneously preparing lunch, which consists of throwing cut up organic potatoes, organic onions and organic turkey sausage in a cast iron skillet. Flavored with Tony Chachere's Original Creole Seasoning — it's "Great on everything!" — organic sea salt, organic black pepper and organic extra virgin olive oil, as well as two organic eggs to hold it all together, it makes for a quick meal. I eat it in under five minutes at my desk.

Lunch is followed by more emails and a phone interview with a local source regarding dog poop. Turns out, according to the anonymous deep throat, dogs are defecating on public pathways at a normal rate this year. It's the shithead owners who aren't picking up after their pets. After this information I end my investigation into dog poop.

At one point before logging off this Monday, I glance at a hand-written sticky note near my keyboard.

"Isolation is a gift. Everything else is just a test of endurance."
—Bukowski

There is an idea of a typical work-from-home day, but while we can talk about the endless Zoom calls and dressed down attire and might think our work lives are comparable even, there is simply nothing typical about it.

WHAT A DIFFERENCE A
YEAR MAKES

The one-year anniversary of the COVID-19 pandemic, and how it drastically changed our day-to-day lives here in San Miguel County, recently passed. It feels like only a week ago, but I clearly remember when Telluride schools shifted to remote learning, our company decided everyone should work from home and county officials declared a state of emergency in less than seven days in March 2020. Do you remember that week? That was not long after the ski season ended abruptly with Governor Jared Polis's statewide decision to shut them down early, the virus dealing a sucker punch that caught many by surprise.

There were more questions than answers at that time. *How quickly does this virus spread? What's the best way to prevent infection? How fatal is it?*

Reflecting on it all now, it's been a blur. One day I was sitting in an emergency county meeting in the Miramonte Building, the next I was downloading an app I had never heard of before. I consider myself a Zoom pro now, but I still don't necessarily prefer it to face-to-face meetings. In covering it all, there wasn't much time to think or contemplate or debate; we simply adapted and learned on the fly. My coworkers and I dove into all the information available at the time. We tracked the spread in other areas, particularly the devastation it was wreaking in Europe early on. We focused on understanding the metrics and how they were reported. We even discussed how to stylize "COVID-19." But we also worried. We worried about what would happen to our community, to our friends, to our family, especially those living in places where the pandemic became politicized to the detriment of public health.

How long will this last? Is the county going to shut down to everyone but locals? What does this mean for the economy? When can we hug one another again?

Main Street fell silent, as businesses shuttered in an effort to prevent the spread. A summer slate barren of all festivals and live entertainment struck us right in the gut, dealing the biggest blow to event producers and venues that had to shift to livestreaming, if nothing else. Another one-two punch from our invisible enemy.

Chris Parente of Denver's Channel 2 recently reached out to me about a piece he was working on regarding newspaper headlines during the pandemic. Our chat went well, and at one point, he asked me what headline stuck out as the one, the biggest, that meant this virus meant business. I thought about the March 16, 2020, state of emergency declaration, as well as the announcement of the first official positive case days later on March 19, but I kept returning to April 9, 2020 — "Bluegrass Festival canceled for the first time ever, largest annual music gathering falls victim to COVID-19."

In Telluride, Bluegrass is more than an annual music festival, I told him, it's an ever-growing community of Festivarians. Losing that summer solstice celebration, along with other sunny season staples, was sobering.

But we picked ourselves up off the mat, hoped for the best and planned for the worst. Little did anyone know then that we'd go a full 365 days under uncertain circumstances, as public health orders shifted with the burden of the virus. But our local officials, particularly in public health, have been nothing short of amazing. No one necessarily predicted that we'd have the vaccine availability we do now, or the amount of ongoing free testing that's been offered throughout the last 12 months, but in seeing how it all came together to lead us to this point, I feel fortunate to call this place home. There's not enough space here to recognize and thank everyone properly for what they've done for the community. From the health care workers tirelessly working every day on the frontlines, to the local governments that created housing relief programs for those in need, and that's not to mention the numerous random acts of kindness that may have gone mostly unnoticed, it's been inspiring to see how everyone rallied for one another.

We should all be proud. We're tougher than we may have previously thought. A new ski season started with stipulations in place to manage capacity, but has gone well by all accounts. Bluegrass seems likely to return in some form or fashion. Local businesses have been slowly navigating reopening without any major hiccups.

A year of body blows behind us and we're still here fighting the good fight, a little more embattled, of course, but life has a way of doing that. At least now there's a brighter light at the end of this long tunnel.

In an open letter to the community, county public health director Grace Franklin and Dr. Sharon Grundy, two of the stalwart local heroes throughout all of this, encourage everyone to stay the course, as we all continue to work toward restoring some sense of normalcy.

"Let's continue to move forward and be the best we can be.

We have seen so much good come from our residents and, although this has been an incredibly difficult year, we have become stronger together. We will continue to persevere."

They close with, "Thinking of all of you."

OFFSEASON OUTINGS

O ffseason is when the weary typically leave for far-flung places and exotic excursions. Conversations around this time of year often include questions about travel plans, as seemingly everyone takes an offseason vacation, if for no other reason than to recalibrate and escape the box canyon for some much-needed time away after yet another busy winter.

Last year, as the COVID-19 pandemic announced its presence stateside, offseason in Telluride was effectively canceled. Officials urged caution and instituted stay-at-home orders. The unknowns of the pandemic kept everyone in place, panicky and uncertain. Businesses, particularly restaurants, that also usually close for at least a couple of weeks each April, stayed open to serve locals who remained here.

No one needs to be reminded of how dreadful 2020 was . But 2021 feels a little different so far; at least offseason does.

San Miguel County is currently tops in the state when it comes to administering vaccines. People are even cautiously using the word "normal" to describe this April. The mass offseason exodus started soon after Closing Day, which ended a successful ski season, given the circumstances. The streets are now barren, aside from a handful of locals who regularly line up outside Coffee Cowboy each morning. Hand-written closure signs dangle from most storefronts with notes explaining tentative timelines for reopening. This is to say that April offseason outings have returned.

After receiving my second vaccination shot, I recently took an offseason vacation myself, as my parents and sister flew in from Pittsburgh for five days. I'm usually working when they're in town, but I took some time off, so we'd be able to adventure more together this visit.

We took day trips to Ouray, Silverton and Mesa Verde National Park — all places they've never been before. We relaxed at the Ouray Hot Springs and even left slightly sunburnt. We drove Red Mountain Pass, stopping along the way to take in the views, including the ghost town of Red Mountain. In Silverton, which is similar to Telluride in population at the moment, we enjoyed walking the sleepy Main Street and stopped at a brewery for lunch. Mesa Verde, though not completely open, couldn't have been better, as the views of Ancestral Puebloan dwellings are always awe-inspiring.

Dad also brought out some records he recently came across, including original pressings of The Stooges's self-titled 1969 debut and follow-up, 1970's "Fun House." Little did he know "The Stooges" had long been one of my holy grails. The sound quality of the record is still great, as there are no scratches or crackling. We all proceeded to dance poorly to "1969" while making dinner one night. It was a nice start to my offseason respite.

After they left, I flew to Scottsdale, Arizona, to visit a friend from Telluride who recently moved there. What a different world. It's a land that the coronavirus apparently never visited.

Though mask mandates are in place at most businesses, rarely does anyone bother to wear one, let alone enforce them.

We went to a bar that leaned more towards a nightclub one night. There were two DJs playing music from their Macbooks, fog machines and a dance floor full of people. We sat at a table to the side of all the commotion. The style, which I assume is in vogue, made me laugh and confirmed that I am completely out of touch with what is currently considered "cool" in the real world. I might be crazy, but everyone looked the same. The guys, who weighed no more than 125 pounds, wore jogger pants and oversized tall tees. Mere scarecrows dressed like popular white rappers Post Malone and Logic. The wardrobe of the women was more diverse, but they were all varying versions of the latest social media influencer at their collective core, including cellphones glued to their dominant hands for "candid" photo opportunities. I call this pop culture devolution the Kardashian Effect.

Too many pretty people in one place freaks me out, and then it hit me, humans are no better than peacocks in this respect, though we've evolved beyond tail feathers and created collagen injections to alter our unwanted faces and thin lips. I wasn't the only one to notice this. My friend and I had a good time realizing we're thirtysomethings who are past our primes.

Before the long weekend ended, I made my buddy take me to Asylum Records in the nearby city of Chandler, which was more my speed. The spot is a metalhead haven. Owner Scott Robenalt ran security for the likes of Metallica and Kiss, as well as Ozzfest, over the years. Man, does he have stories, and the memorabilia to back them up. While I flipped through vinyl, Robenalt talked about the giant black pentagram that bisected his shop. It belonged to Wendy O. Williams and the Plasmatics. Used for the cover of the band's 1981 album "Metal Priestess," the prop was featured on stage during the subsequent tour.

When I brought my finds to the counter — two original vinyl variants and a cassette of Judas Priest's 1981 record "Point of Entry;" Anthrax's 1990 "Persistence of Time" on cassette; Dimebag Darrell's "The Hitz," a 2017 Record Store Day exclusive vinyl; and B.B. King's 1970 "Indianola Mississippi Seeds" record — Robenalt pulled out a picture of himself and Dimebag.

"This was the last time I saw him alive," he said of the guitar god who was gunned down on stage Dec. 8, 2004, in Columbus, Ohio, while playing with his new band Damageplan. "He was my buddy."

I could have stayed there all day listening to his heavy metal shenanigans, but the best thing about my offseason vacation was how normal it all felt.

MOVIE NIGHT

Raise your hand if you miss going to the movies. Yeah, every cinephile does. The longstanding ritual of deciding on a show time, arriving early enough to buy a ticket, before heading to the concession counter for a drink and snacks, and finding a seat that's not too close or too far away from the screen has been rendered a distant memory by the pandemic.

But as everything is slowly but surely reopening, I'm getting excited about seeing a new release in a theater. There's nothing quite like that experience. The dimming of lights. The low rumble of the bass as the previews start. Situating your napkins in an open cup holder just right. Maybe there's an empty seat in front of you, so go ahead and throw your legs over it. Lean back, relax and finish all your refreshments before the movie starts.

Movie theater popcorn has a distinct flavor that can't be replicated. Maybe the secret is pouring so much salt on it that your tongue shrivels up like a slug, the only antidote being a cherry-blue raspberry Icee that turns your brain into an iceberg. Yeah, I'm jonesing for it. Pro tip: Buy a bag of peanut M&M's and sprinkle them on top of your bag of warm popcorn. An ex showed me that trick during one of our dates. I can't recall the movie we saw. We broke it off shortly after that night. I'll be forever grateful for that movie theater recipe, but I can't eat peanut M&M's over popcorn without thinking of her and how she looked that night. Who knew ghosts could haunt such a fun food.

The last wide release I saw in a theater was "Once Upon A Time... In Hollywood" at the Nugget during the summer of 2019. I'm only now realizing that's almost two years ago.

But while we all patiently await the reopening of our beloved local theater, as well as the return of Mountainfilm, Telluride Film Festival and Telluride Horror Show, my friends and I have been holding movie nights.

Yes, movies. The word itself makes some snobs cringe with disgust, but these gatherings are far from sophisticated "film screenings." The idea sprang up prior to the recent release of "Mortal Kombat," which was only available to stream on HBO Max.

The remake is rated R, so it's not for kids, but the millennials who grew up with the video games and original movies in the 1990s. It's fascinating what the developing mind retains. My friends and I can still recall characters, their signature moves, including fatalities and "animalities" (characters morph into animals to kill their opponents), cheat codes, and the storyline. We know who is supposed to be good and bad and kick butt and stuff. But we also knew going in that Scorpion, one of the baddest fighters north of hell, was a good guy. *No way*. And he has a descendant who is a brand new character. *Stop*. Yeah, we were intrigued all right.

My buddy Big Steve (he's tall) hosted the viewing. I brought the snacks — a DiGiorno deep dish pizza, Totino's Pizza Rolls and Jose Olé Taquitos. We cooked up the goods, smoked some indica and melted into the couch like the poor girl in that 1990s anti-marijuana PSA. Yeah, we were ready.

To avoid too many spoilers, all I'll say is "Mortal Kombat" delivered. The more "mature" rating meant more realistic gore (read buckets of blood), and allowed Kano, the Australian leader of the Black Dragon group who shoots a laser beam out of his right eye, to carry the movie with his profanity-laced insults and back-stabbing antics.

Afterward, we nerded out in picking apart the finer details. OK, spoiler alert.

They never really did hold the Mortal Kombat tournament.

Goro, who was a four-armed unstoppable force in the 1990s, got gutted like a pig by the new guy, whose power is ... a magic bracelet that covers his body in armor made of golden thread whenever he's angry.

Raiden, the lightning-wielding God of Thunder, didn't electrocute enough people, particularly Shang Tsung, who only sucked one person's soul out of their mouth. Poor, Kung Lao.

Kabal sounded like a frat bro from New Jersey, which only reminded us of our friend from the Garbage State.

And who the hell is General Reiko?

But I digress. We all thoroughly enjoyed it, as the ending left it open to a sequel or seven.

The following weekend, we found ourselves back at Steve's. Street tacos were on the menu, and the bill included cheesy 1980s horror movies, mainly the 1984 Troma classic "The Toxic Avenger." If you have never seen this movie, stop reading right now and go watch it. You will not be disappointed. It's thick with 1980s tropes, including emotionless bullies who like to run over innocent civilians in their Camaro and pick on the pencil-necked geek at the local gym, in turn creating Toxie. Is he a vigilante hero or a mutated monster murderer? You decide.

The second feature that night was Peter Jackson's 1987 zany horror-comedy "Bad Taste," which we found by mistake. We wanted to watch Jackson's "Dead Alive," but in our altered state, we landed on his alien-zombie-what-the-hell-is-going-on debut.

It might have been the bud, but in this case, Jackson's aversion to brevity doesn't make the film any better, though special effects, which include a man constantly shoving his brains into the back of his head, were endearing.

Yeah, our movie nights might not include the creature comforts of a proper theater, but it's a temporary cure for our cinephilia during a time filled with more gore than most movies.

FESTIVAL OF FREAKS

After a year off, the return of summer festivals also marks the return of the many "Festivarians" that travel in hordes across the country seeking satisfying sounds. Whether that's bluegrass music or not is irrelevant to me. Until death metal, or any subgenre heavier than hard rock, graces Telluride Town Park, I'll always be more interested in people watching during this particular season.

Like many of us who live here, I have a service industry side hustle running security for a handful of local watering holes, particularly during busier festival weekends throughout the summer.

While my coworkers handled the Telluride Bluegrass Festival coverage like the pros they are throughout the first weekend, I focused my attention on the nocturnal festival of freaks.

The nefarious world of barflies and otherwise altered hippies is best experienced as a sober bystander, and a bar bouncer has a free front row seat to the show after the Town Park stage falls silent.

The profession requires one to take in their surroundings

with the mindset that a free-for-all bar fight may break out at any moment, but hippies don't like to throw punches, I've discovered through my on-the-job observations. They may feel brave at a certain hour and shout obscenities, or even tip over a barstool and create a mini-ruckus, but they're innately docile creatures, which makes my job that much easier, as I'm more of a presence, an ominous shadow of sorts, than a bare-knuckled enforcer.

Temper tantrums aside, the job allows me to freely mingle amongst the freaks. There are the oldheads who barely stay out past midnight anymore, the better days of their youth and partying well behind them, though they still have the hunger to be part of the scene and test their stamina every year for no other reason than to say they can still hang, even if they'll pay for it the next morning.

Then there's the new breed, a more interesting collection of direct descendants who grew up around the twang and tinge of it all, and the others who were cosmically inclined to make the pilgrimage into the mountains during this time of year, even if they only end up playing their instruments around campfires in the pale moonlight, or on empty street corners with hopes of filling their cups with enough loose change to get another drink or slice of pizza for the night.

It's the younger ones who keep the scene alive and thriving, while the elders are more than happy to impart their wisdom through stories of festivals and bad trips past.

The blackness during these late nights veils most, but it also reveals a great deal. Some tips and tales I overheard during Bluegrass included how to properly navigate the campground scene without coming off like a newb, mainly don't ask what the camp hosts are offering you, just take it.

I found myself in a similar situation while wandering the strange shantytown as a rookie in search of a story my first year in town. Stopping at different camps during my journey, I eventually stumbled upon Hippie Jerry's Camp Run-A-Muck. Jerry, the elder gentleman responsible for bringing together Bluegrass fans with nicknames like Hot Sugar and Hooch, built a must-see camp, complete with a strange alcoholic drink called Crunchy Frog that tastes like vodka and lemonade, though the camp elders won't say what's in it. They've taken a blood oath, I was told. But they did break out "wax," which I'd never smoked at that point. I didn't ask question and hit the tube after the glass plate was heated up with a blow torch.

The middle-aged man in charge of the wax said, "Woah, that was a big hit." I did two more before my body started melting from the feet up. By the time I left the campground and made my way to a local bar, I could barely sit up in my chair. I slept in my car that night, but it was a lesson learned.

Drugs are a crucial, if not the most important, aspect of the festival of freaks. I overheard one old head tell a young man clad in denim and dancing bears not to eat too much acid before noon, when the sun is reaching its hottest. You'll feel like an egg in a frying pan, the senior said.

A deranged "Durangotan," as he proclaimed his citizenry of Durango, matter-of-factly stated, "Oh, yeah, I'm weird. I'm a weirdo."

He had an unnatural look in his eye that I interpreted as the unfocused glare of good times. But he was harmless, I quickly concluded. While chatting him up later in the night, I discovered he's a fellow Keystoner. His family still owns and operates a kielbasa company in eastern Pennsylvania.

"Best kielbasa in the country," he said of his ancestor's Polish recipe.

Around the same time, a friend walked in. Exhausted from a long weekend of festival festivities, she decided to have one more drink before calling it a weekend.

She described an alien interaction she recently had. After eating a tab of good acid from a stranger in the campground, she was forced to make small talk as the world around her fell apart and reconstructed itself in bizarre ways. Twenty minutes into a meaningless conversation with a woman who she had just met, my friend explained she couldn't take anymore and interrupted.

"Ma'am, you have no face."

The woman, who most likely did have all the standard facial features of our species, repeatedly apologized, but my friend had to walk away and collect herself. She sat at the end of the bar by herself. She ordered that last drink, but barely touched it. Her eyes were more focused on her hands folded in her lap. Survival, not revelry, became her focus.

There is a fine line between free-spirited fun and unparalleled fear. The paradox with this is one often doesn't realize there is a line, let alone when it's crossed, until the darkness takes over. This phenomenon physically manifests itself in the eyes. The pupils, which dilate to various abnormal circumferences, fill with doubt, paranoia, mistrust and terror. Reality becomes a question of the senses.

Are the walls really dripping wet with blood?
Why does everyone look like a Picasso painting?
What is the point of a pinky toe if you can't feel it?

The senses start playing tricks on you. I once ate acid in public only to find myself sitting in a Paris café full of cannibals. The red neon lights from the bar's beer signs painted my world in a sinister shade. I needed to leave immediately before the people around me satiated their taste for flesh. I scurried home, but that posed another problem — my modified mind convinced me I was being tailed by a pack of wild dogs. I refused to look back and outran the phantom hounds. I slept in my car that night, but it was a lesson learned.

Knowing the visual deformities that accompany such trips, I like to imagine a person of my height and weight, who is covered in tattoos and has the furrowed brow of a Cro-Magnon, appears more like an Orc to those mired in that state of mind.

But despite the gloominess and excessive consumption of substances during this festival of freaks, I've realized we are all here searching for the same thing, or at least the feeling of the same thing. What that exactly is, I cannot tell you at this point in my journey, but we achieve it along our own personal paths and through experiences along the way.

As Thomas Ligotti wrote in the "The Conspiracy Against the Human Race," a nonfiction collection of his essays on human existence, "If truth is what you seek, then the examined life will only take you on a long ride to the limits of solitude and leave you by the side of the road with your truth and nothing else."

A SAILOR'S GRAVE

There's nothing like a marina in the morning. As the sun rises, the waters come to life. People stir and awaken from moored yachts with names like "Two Tickets" and "Sandy Cheeks," while those with smaller single-engine boats arrive for fuel and supplies before starting their day.

I found myself observing such a scene during a family vacation in the U.S. Virgin Islands. We stayed on St. Thomas, but took ferries to Water Island and St. John for day-trips. Early for our 10-minute boat ride from Charlotte Amalie to Water Island, I had time to take in the sights and sounds of one of the island's busiest boatyards.

At one point, a shirtless man with skin like leather arrived in his motorized dinghy. He docked near the Water Island ferry, but before he unloaded, he took out his short-sleeved button-up and belt, got dressed, fixed his hair in the reflection of his sunglasses, and then made his way to a nearby restaurant for breakfast, where he was welcomed by a similar sea-salt siren. I imagined the waitress served him the usual plate of seaweed and locally caught crustaceans, which he munched on without hesitation before diving into the nearby waters to start his day as a barnacle-sucking boat cleaner.

An older woman in a small boat pulled up alongside the walkway and met a man with a wheelbarrow full of soft drinks and bottled water. It looked like a low-level drug deal. I wondered what was really in those cans of Coke. The best smugglers keep a low profile, or so I've heard. She loaded up the liquid, waved goodbye and took off in the opposite direction. The closest land that way was St. Croix. Beyond that lie Aruba and Venezuela. I imagined she tore off her grandma wig and accompanying wrinkled mask once there was no land in sight, as she headed toward a destination that promised a big payday, only if she could make the journey in such an unequipped vessel. What a commute, I thought.

Seagulls cawed in chaotic communication. It must be mating season, or there's a serious territory dispute at this particular marina. The people who frequent the area would be collateral damage if the seagulls where to battle. The birds are known to eat each other and small animals, including dogs, if nothing else. Rations of human flesh may support the ongoing war effort.

As the seagull scene crossed my mind, a pelican dove into the shallow waters near the dock for fish. Such strong and intelligent birds would be an ally during the wharf war. The humans may stand a chance after all. This is the life aquatic.

With all of this happening around me, I daydreamed of faking my own death, pirating a boat and sailing the open sea. I'd hop around the spate of Caribbean islands, scavenge for food and drink, and when I felt like walking on solid ground, I'd anchor off the shores of one of the many uninhabited cays and make myself at home. Maybe I'd fall in with a band of corsair castaways and ungovernable buccaneers.

I wouldn't mind running barrels of rum and gun powder.

The Grandma Smuggler and I would have a good working relationship. If authorities found out about my Blackbeard ways, I'd lead them to the sharks, slice my palms open with a salt-rusted saber and blow a hole through my bow. I don't know much about boats, but I do know the captain always goes down with the ship.

Unfortunately, the islands aren't quite that lawless anymore, as tourism is one of area's biggest economies, aside from rum production and exports.

Visitors are welcomed at the Cyril E. King Airport with dancers on stilts and steel-drum music, a caricature of the culture that mainlanders have come to expect.

I arrived at the airport a couple hours before my family, so I found a spot in the rear of a small bar near baggage claim. A Black man with a friendly face and a New York Yankees hat greeted me.

"Dealer's choice," I told him.

"I got just the thing for you," he said, before mixing Tampico juice and a splash of rum. "Rum punch! ... $12."

It didn't take long for the humidity to cover my body in a layer of moisture. I felt slimy like a lizard from the moment I got off the plane until I left. This is the life aquatic.

Staying in Megans Bay on the north side of St. Thomas, we spent most of our time at the beach there. On the second day, we drank so much that my sister, Karlee, lost her engagement ring in the ocean. She didn't care, though, since the rubber ring she wears most of the time was hardly buried treasure.

Between beverages, we snorkeled the shallows. Baby blacktip sharks hung out near the shore at certain times. They're about two-feet long and fast as hell. We saw a couple swim around our legs, but they weren't too close, until one headbutted Karlee's ass. We were done for the day.

Similarly, while visiting Trunk Bay on St. John later in the week, we snorkeled for hours. We must have covered 10 miles. There were stingrays, barracudas, tarpons and jellyfish, not to mention thousands of tropical fish. The schools engulfed us almost immediately. At one point, I became lost in one of these breathing blankets, taking in the colors and movements, but when I pushed through the other side, I discovered a five-foot blacktip shark. Luckily, it was swimming away from us, but then I realized it must have spotted us before we noticed it.

I love sharks and have swum with them in a controlled environment before, but seeing one in the wild was one of the most exciting, yet startling, moments of my life.

We surfaced and processed what we had just seen. Snorkelers nearby heard our disbelief and quickly took over the area, but the blacktip was long gone by then. We were done for the day, but I imagined being chewed up and buried in the belly of such a strong sea creature in marauder martyrdom. This is the life aquatic.

We finished our visit to St. John at nearby Maho Bay Beach, which is known for its sea turtles. Watching a sea turtle chomp on seaweed is much more relaxing than swimming with sharks.

The time on the islands melted away too fast. But it always does. While traveling back to the mainland, which required an overnight stay in Denver, reality crept back in.

Do I have enough toilet paper?

Why is my July electric bill so high?

How long should I wait before I take another vacation?

I know the islands, marina, birds, bootleggers, Karlee's ring, sea turtles and sharks will always be there, but as I sat on my return flight, sunburnt and sullen, a sailor's grave is all I craved.

A WALK-OFF WIN

After five years in Colorado, I finally made my way to Coors Field for a Rockies baseball game. Since moving West, I've heard nothing but good things about the mile-high stadium that opened in 1995, only two years after the team itself was created.

I grabbed a press pass for a recent Saturday night game, as I was already planning to be in town for a death metal show. Owen Perkins, a former Tellurider and our newspaper's current Rockies writer, helped me with the credentials. He showed me the ropes and introduced me to the other sportswriters who cover the sport. There's an inherent drama about the game that can bring a lightning-struck tree or homemade field in Iowa to life, and the people who write about it for a living know that.

Sportswriters are fans as much as they are pros, many living childhood dreams of being around the game they grew up loving. They talk about stats and share war stories, as if they were directly involved in the outcomes of legendary baseball diamond battles. Originally from Charm City, Owen told me about how he was at Game 7 of the 1971 World Series between the Pittsburgh Pirates and Baltimore Orioles. He and his family

weren't sitting in their regular seats at Baltimore's old Memorial Stadium. When a young Owen asked why, his dad told him
this was their one chance to see Roberto Clemente, the Pirates
right fielder who became an all-time great before his sudden
death in 1972. The right field wall in PNC Park, the current
home of the Pirates, is 21-feet high in honor of Clemente, who
wore number 21 during his 18 seasons in the Steel City. It felt
good to be back inside a Major League press box.

Due to a weather delay, I had time to walk around Coors
Field, including visiting the popular Rooftop and Rockpile
areas, and stopped at an ice cream booth to fill up a souvenir
batting helmet bowl before first pitch.

"Load it up," the young man working the ice cream stand
said after going over a list of toppings. Tall and sinewy, he
looked like a centerfielder whose diet wouldn't consist of eating
dairy products out of such a childish keepsake.

I started with a mound of chocolate-vanilla swirl ice cream.
Then I added a spoonful of crumbled Oreo cookies and mini-
M&M's. A dash of sprinkles gave my creation some color.
Chocolate is my biggest vice, so I drizzled Hershey syrup over
top of it all.

First pitch approached, so I made my way back to the press
box with the helmet full of dessert.

"That your first batting helmet?" a sportswriter around my
age asked.

"No, but it's the first one in a while," I said remembering a
childhood that included collecting such bowls.

The nostalgia surrounding baseball may be the main
reason why it's still America's pastime, even though football
has become king in terms of ratings and revenue. Walking
through the ballpark, the banners and snapshots of past
glories are shown proudly. The history forever having a front
row seat. Adults and kids alike bring their baseball gloves to

games in hopes of being a part of the action, whether it's catching a homerun or foul ball. We're a nation of former Little Leaguers waiting for the call up to the Big Show, no matter how many years it's been since we stepped into a batter's box.

As a baseball nerd and former sportswriter, PNC Park is still the most beautiful stadium in the big leagues, but Coors Field is right up there. PNC Park must be more beautiful than anything, since the teams that have played there over the past two decades have been little more than hot trash, sans the three-straight National League Wild Card teams from 2013-15.

I covered the Buccos during the 2013 regular season. No one expected them to sneak into the playoffs before the season, though they had talent like Andrew McCutchen, who went on to win the MVP that season, and power-hitting third baseman Pedro Alvarez. Lead by manager Clint Hurdle, who wasn't far removed from a 2007 World Series run with the Rockies, the Pirates snapped the longest losing streak in North American sports history when they finished over .500 for the first time in 20 years. Yes, Rockies fans, it can always be worse.

A game between the Rockies and Arizona Diamondbacks during the dog days of summer, while both are sharing a spot in the basement of the NL West division, isn't necessarily a high-stakes affair, but don't tell that to the 32,699 diehards in attendance that night. The crowd responded to the scoreboard's calls for "two strike noise" and sung along to Charlie Blackmon's walk-up song — The Outfield's "Your Love" — by finishing with a resounding "tonight!" every time he approached the plate. It felt like a postseason game.

Plus, the Rox have been playing good ball at home and flirting with .500 since the All-Star Game in July, which was held at Coors Field and a grand success, by all accounts. The Saturday night game turned out to be as dramatic as any, complete with a walk-off homerun in the bottom of the ninth with two outs and the Rockies down to their last strike.

Rockies starting pitcher Kyle Freeland struck out 10, which tied a career high, and allowed two earned runs before he exited after the seventh, but Arizona's Zac Gallen quelled the Colorado bats in allowing three hits over seven innings, including nine strikeouts.

But the Rox were able to take advantage of the bullpen after Gallen's exit. Pinch hitter Garrett Hampson hit a two-run homer in the bottom of the eighth to tie the game at 2-2, which set the stage for the exciting finish.

Catcher Elias Díaz saw 10 pitches during the game's final at-bat, and he kept pulling it down the left field line.

No cheering in the press box is one of the cardinal rules of sports reporting, but it's impossible not to comment on a game. Owen and I sat there during the ninth and speculated on how it might end.

"He likes that corner," I said. "If he hits it down there, it's game over."

With no more outs to give, Blackmon took a generous lead off of second before each pitch. You could almost feel the fans holding their collective breathe. With every foul ball during Díaz's plate appearance, the faithful would jump up and cheer like the Rox won the World Series, before quickly quieting down and settling in for another pitch, just to do it all over again. Blackmon looked like a track star at each crack of the bat, as Díaz fouled off six pitches from reliever J.B. Wendelken, who took the loss. To the fans, that was the equivalent of six mini-heart attacks. Finally, Díaz took advantage of a slider that Wendelken hung too high and sent it over the leftfield fence, where a fan who finally got their shot in a big league game made a nice catch.

Blackmon didn't have to sprint home, but instead jogged

across home plate for the winning run. His Rockies teammates were there to welcome him, as well as Díaz, with a shower of waving water bottles and Dubble Bubble gum.

Díaz wore the empty chewing gum bucket on his head like a crown, as he received high-fives and hugs from teammates. No matter the stakes, he was king for a night.

The stadium erupted in a synchronized roar, before the fans wandered into the night happy. They'd eventually settle down and forget the circumstances surrounding the game, but they'll remember that feeling of elation the Rockies provided during the Saturday night spectacle. That is the inherent drama of baseball.

ZOMBIE WALTZ

While festivals and social gatherings have returned, there has been a less popular, if not entirely unknown, event taking place along Main Street nearly every night as well. This free show hasn't been advertised or well attended, but I believe it's the most interesting to experience.

Each night, particularly during busier weekends, around the witching hour of 3 a.m. there's a mass exodus of weary service industry workers who can finally make their way home in conducting a zombie waltz of sorts across Colorado Avenue. It's not a celebration by any means, but the result of surviving another night on the frontlines and fighting the urge to gnaw on the faces of the humans who bark and moan at them about mask mandates and related virus metrics. While the true corpses enviously rest in Lone Tree Cemetery, the local living dead can finally breathe a sigh of relief at that time under the veil of night. Their hunger to devour those so full of blood and ignorance only grows harder to ignore with each shift that passes. Cigarettes and cocaine help, but the body wants what it wants.

As a doorman I've partaken in this Danse Macabre. The bars close. The usual gush of people stumbling and crawling about town like bloated worms after an evening thunderstorm follows, maybe there's some loud shouting and a threat of a drunken fight among the mortals. But the zombies could care less. They must clean and restock for the next day before calling it a night.

After the streets are clear of stupefied people, the zombies emerge, heads down, feet dragging. We decompress by chatting about how our nights went and share war stories.

"How'd it go tonight?"

"We got a rush at midnight when the show let out, but then it slowed down. I had to throw a girl out after she jumped on the bar."

"Did you see the guy with the Houston Astros hat? He couldn't even talk."

"Yeah, I didn't let him in. He just seemed like a douche."

"But did you see how meaty his thighs were?"

"Don't even think about it. Go home."

"Yeah, the booze probably makes it taste bad."

Some need more time to process such thoughts and find refuge wherever they can.

"I'm gonna go down to the dungeon and hang out with the vampires."

I typically head home on these nights. Nothing good happens between dusk and dawn, unless you're looking for some type of sin. If you're up early enough, you may catch a vampire, sniffling and spastic, dragging themselves back to their coffins before the morning sun renders them a pile of ash and white powder.

If I'm lucky, I'll scavenge some leftover pizza during my shift and save it until I get back to my place. It's not human flesh, but it holds me over. Sitting there alone, hunched over and wretched, with only my black cat's eye to witness the carnage, I imagine biting into someone's cheek whenever I chomp on a slice of cold pizza at 3:30 a.m. on a Saturday. I rip away each bite with a quick twitch of the head, sliding it down my throat and swallowing like a ravenous bird. The toughened texture and the way the red sauce squirts from between the cheese and crust into the corners of my mouth temporarily satiates my bloodlust. But pretending to be a people-eater with prepared foods won't last much longer.

Enforcing the indoor mask ordinance has turned even the most congenial among us into brain-craving cannibals. A man and woman stopped at the doorway recently and peaked into the bar. I told them that we ask everyone to wear a mask when they enter until they order a drink and find their seat. The man saw the signs posted in the windows and looked at me like I'd just ate his first-born.

"We're from Nebraska, where logic lives," he said, before informing me on how virus transmission actually works, and the local mandates are doing nothing to stop the spread of a contagion as harmless as the common flu.

Albert Camus once said, "As I usually do when I want to get rid of someone whose conversation bores me, I pretend to agree." That applies to most of my interactions at the bar.

The Cornhusker couple didn't come in after our chat, but I've agreed with a lot of people recently. If only they knew the visions are becoming more vivid and violent. Even after eating my nightly ration of fleshy pizza, my stomach still growls.

I asked my old friend Scarecrow how someone can talk without brains.

"I don't know," he said. "But some people without brains do an awful lot of talking ... don't they?"

No wonder why zombies only want to eat the living.

One night, after the beer was cooling in the fridge and the

doors were locked, the three bartenders and I sat on a bench outside and leaned against the wall to smoke American Spirits before going our separate ways. We didn't speak other than to ask one another for a light. The moment lasted no more than five minutes, but during that time, we were all unburdening ourselves. Tired and beleaguered, we said our goodbyes.

"See ya tomorrow."

George Romero couldn't have framed a better shot.

Some nights it seems like even the flies won't befriend us, but for those who make their living in the service industry, there is no other option than to push on.

As a result, another strange phenomenon I've noticed this year is that no one is talking about leaving the canyon for exotic offseason vacations. Bali and Thailand can wait. Most people simply want some time to do nothing and recalibrate before the winter rolls in.

When you live in one place long enough it becomes three-dimensional. Once the veil is pierced and the innards behind it are exposed, there's no going back.

The hardworking zombies know this, so if you happen to witness their waltz one night, dear reader, please don't intervene or mock them. An extra couple dollars as appreciation for their long hours or just treating them with respect is all they may crave.

BEER AND BLOATING

L as Vegas is a modern-day Sodom and Gomorrah, but there is nothing religious or profound about it, as the city of the desert perpetually festers in its excesses and decadence without intervention or destruction from above.

Ever since Hunter S. Thompson romanticized Sin City and its innate vice in his seminal 1971 work "Fear and Loathing in Las Vegas: A Savage Journey to the Heart of the American Dream," every bachelor with a few bucks in his pocket and a penchant for mind-altering substances has been willingly visiting Nevada with a head full of perverted fantasies in trying to recreate some of the debauchery described in Thompson's fever dream of a book.

But the secret's out. The place that was a swanky getaway for Hollywood stars whenever Thompson descended upon it with a suitcase full of hard drugs and an eye for the weird has mutated into a destination for people who enjoy cruise ships and $20 cocktails in flamingo-shaped cups. If only the scent of sulfur lingered in the air instead of piss and booze-laced sweat.

Now everyone has a Las Vegas story about some degenerate act of humanity. The truth is you can party and lose money anywhere, but for whatever reason it's more acceptable there, if not encouraged. The group of housewives taking a girls trip hooting and hollering at a poker table as they gamble away their families' savings. The older men on a business trip eying girls half their age with wicked thoughts of disgusting sexual acts. It's all celebrated in Las Vegas, a place where a man who is slowly eating himself to death can make a career out of being "Big Elvis."

These thoughts crossed my mind as I sat on a plane back to Colorado after a recent weekend trip there with a couple of friends.

While most amateurs who travel Las Vegas are interested in huffing ether and wearing aviator sunglasses, we were hell bent for leather, and the only way for us to sate our heavy metal hunger was to see Judas Priest live and in the flesh. But God had other plans. Priest guitarist Richie Faulkner suffered a medical emergency, and the band canceled the rest of the tour before the Vegas date. Thankfully, he survived and is expected to make a full recovery. We adjusted our plans and decided to checkout Sin City Slaughterfest one night and ZZ Top the next. There's always something to do in Las Vegas.

We stayed in a seedy two-star motel on the Strip that was built above a liquor store and behind a tattoo shop. While the concerts we saw were great, we spent a lot of time hanging out near our hotel amongst the horrors of the Strip.

The relentless waves of humanity that flood Las Vegas Boulevard South each day are filled with toothless show girls who beg people to take pictures with them for money, frat boys who can't hold their liquor and stagger about thinking they're in "The Hangover," and obese couples wearing matching Raiders jerseys and wedgies. And people in Telluride think long lift lines are hell.

Not to mention the noise, my God, the noise is a never-ending cacophony of chaos. From police sirens and loud music to the static hum of a million simultaneous conversations, the voice of Vegas is a harrowing howl. If only the heavens were listening. But the most terrifying part is that's only what's observable on the surface.

Deep in the darkest corners of Las Vegas lives a sadness so severe no one in their right mind wants to recognize it. The broke and disheartened are discarded and eventually become trapped in this inescapable version of hell on Earth. A homeless man sat on one of the walking bridges above the Strip with a sign that read, "Need money 4 drugs n hoes." Further along, I noticed a man with dreads dive into a garbage can and pull out a half-empty iced coffee. He sniffed it, shrugged and took a sip before continuing to rummage for scraps.

One night, while walking home from the ZZ Top show, a hooker with a lazy eye approached me about having some "fun." I acted like I didn't hear her. If only the devil had a better complexion and less heroin tracks along her arms.

During my early morning trip to the airport, I waited for my Uber ride outside on the Strip. It was 3:30 a.m. There weren't hordes of revelers. No show girls or frat boys either.

A man with a bottle of beer in each hand stumbled toward me yelling, "Oh, my God!" repeatedly. He looked homeless, but a couple of nights in Las Vegas will make anyone look like that. I ignored him, but had a strange thought: *Wonder if that's Jesus, and he unknowingly landed in Las Vegas for the Second Coming. But no one believed him, or cared, and he fell victim to this place like so many have over the years.*

This vision reminded me of Genesis 19:17 and the angels that were sent to warn Lot and his family about the fate of Sodom and Gomorrah.

"Escape for thy life; look not behind thee, neither stay thou in all the Plain; escape to the mountain, lest thou be consumed."

As the fallen son came closer, I noticed he was swigging a Budweiser and a Corona. So that's why his blood is booze, I thought. My gaze fell to my phone and the map of the Uber driver's progress. The drunken prophet then tried to enter the tattoo shop, but a security guard came out to stop him.

"You good?" he asked.

"Oh! My! God!"

He continued down the Strip toward the bright lights of the MGM Grand.

I relaxed in knowing I wouldn't have to answer for my transgressions hungover and haggard in Las Vegas. The Bible is filled with fire and brimstone, but as Aldous Huxley once said, "Don't try to behave as though you were essentially sane and naturally good. We're all demented sinners in the same cosmic boat, and the boat is perpetually sinking."

MAN OF STEEL

Mark Twain once called Pittsburgh "a miniature hell with the lid off."

The famous satirist made the remark during an 1884 trip to the Steel City to promote his upcoming book "Adventures of Huckleberry Finn."

"With the moon soft and mellow ... we sauntered about the mount and looked down on the lake of fire and flame. It looked like a miniature hell with the lid off," Twain was quoted in a Dec. 31, 1884, Pittsburgh Post-Gazette story.

He went on to add, "The view is not as deliciously beautiful as one would suppose. If one can be calm and resolute, he can look upon the picture and still live. Otherwise, your city is a beauty."

The fire-filled quip wasn't necessarily an original Twainism, as journalist James Patton had written Pittsburgh was like "hell with the lid taken off" in an Atlantic Monthly magazine story 16 years earlier. As much as things change, they stay the same. Today Pittsburgh and the steel industry are synonymous, even if the view that Twain and Patton gazed upon from Mount Washington more than a century ago is a little different. There are more skyscrapers and sports stadiums, and fewer barges dotting the murky rivers and clouds of smoke crowding the air, but the inside of a steel mill is still a version of hell. The revitalized Rust Belt city is currently home to several plants that continue to work in conjunction to mold and forge good ole' American steel.

My dad has been a crane operator at U.S. Steel's Edgar Thomson plant in Braddock for over a decade now. The 176-acre compound on the banks of the Monongahela River has been producing seemingly nonstop since Andrew Carnegie officially opened it in 1875. As one of the country's first plants to employ the Bessemer process, Edgar Thomson was hailed as "the most perfect establishment of the kind in the world," according to the Pittsburgh Daily Gazette at the time.

Like the Vulcans who came before him, Dad is now part of the plant's rich history. He's responsible for lifting and maneuvering the large ladles that hold the molten liquid, which is essentially manmade lava, from his floating captain's chair in the air as it runs along a track against the mill's ceiling.

The pots are as "big as a house," he's told me, and if someone drops a full one, it'd react similarly to detonating an atomic bomb. These are the same receptacles that killed the Terminator, melting him in minutes, a final thumbs up being the lasting image.

Dad has explained the intricacies of his job and the mill hunk life to me through numerous phone calls over the years, particularly whenever he's on night turn and has more downtime.

During a recent string of overnight shifts, we caught up on everything from Pittsburgh sports and our cats to my parents preparing to move into the new house they recently purchased and upcoming Thanksgiving Day plans.

I recently decided to fly home for the holiday, but Dad had

been scheduled to work that day, which means more pay in the mill industry.

It wouldn't be the first holiday he's missed because of work, but he said he'd ask if anyone would switch shifts with him this Thanksgiving. He put a sticky note up in his crane cabin about it, per steel mill protocol. But as of last week, there were no takers, and the family accepted that he'd miss Thanksgiving dinner at my cousin's this year.

We didn't talk about it much after that. One phone call focused on football. The Baltimore Ravens were losing to the underdog Miami Dolphins. At the same time, the Pitt Panthers football team was in a back-and-forth shootout with North Carolina. Pitt pulled it out in overtime, and the Ravens — the biggest rival of our beloved Steelers — lost.

The mill workers were giving each other score updates over the radios all night.

"Miami 22, Baltimore 10. Final," I heard a staticky voice bark in the background.

Nearly every talking head in the sports world tapped Baltimore as the favorite to win the AFC North this year, while the Steelers were bottom dwellers limping to the finish line with an aging all-time great quarterback in 39-year-old Ben Roethlisberger. He's delivered some of the franchise's most cherished moments, including two Super Bowl titles, in his 18 years under center, but the death rattle of the Roethlisberger era meant we found even more joy in the downfall of foes this season.

The Ravens loss made for a good night, Dad said. He went on to talk about how everyone at the mill has a different radio cadence whenever the ladles were making their way down the line. Some say, "You got it" or "Ladle coming out." Dad typically responses with a simple, "Alright." One guy always says, "Thank you, sir," he explained.

"This ain't a 'sir' type of place," Dad told me.

From what I collect, it's a place where calling someone "ugly" is a term of endearment, and curse words are used as nouns, verbs and adjectives. It's clear that the mill doesn't just mold steel, but a certain type of person, and some people are made a little tougher than others.

If the sheer machinery of a steel mill isn't enough to kill an average person, the conditions it houses will. The ear-splitting sirens. The showers of sparks. The ungodly heat and humidity. The slim margin of error. Death comes in many forms at the mill, but so do superheroes. It's not the mindset of a Pittsburgh steel mill worker to cower at the harsh reality of the mill, but to manage the rigors and weight of a job well done. If it wasn't for them, Carnegie's cutting-edge creation would be no more than an industrial memorial.

I wrote an essay in elementary school about how my dad was my hero. Over 20 years later, he still is, because I know I'd never willingly walk into the hell he has over the years in providing for our family, and he's made sure I never had to.

I was playing my guitar one night and thinking about how cutting a fingertip on a string feels kind of good, when I received a text from Dad.

"Can do Thanksgiving!" he sent to the family group chat.

We all responded with excitement. His coworker who has been off recovering from an injury took the holiday shift because he needs the pay.

That means Dad's next turn is 2 a.m. to 2 p.m. His "penance" for switching out Thanksgiving, he later told me.

"I can give a shit less. I can handle it for a night," he said.

TURN OF THE WORMS

W hile everyone has heard of Christmas miracles, as the holidays approach I must share a tale of a Christmas curse that's so blood-curdling I seriously debated if I should chronicle the details for you hear, wistful reader, or ignore the horrors that have befallen my beloved aunt in hopes it is only a recurring bad dream. I ultimately decided it would do more harm not to make a permanent record of the events, especially if the monsters are as mobile as they appear, for this is something I cannot shake.

In the backwoods of western Pennsylvania, along a scant stretch of earth called Coal Valley, a new breed of horror has found a home. This is no phantasmagoric poltergeist, but a macabre phenomenon of Mother Nature.

My dear aunt, God bless her, is the poor victim of this slithering terror, as her property is overcome with Asian jumping worms.

These are no ordinary night crawlers. The dirt demons can grow up to eight inches in length and are as thick as a thumb. When threatened they violently convulse and "jump" to avoid harm and can even detach their tails in getting away. But the most horrifying characteristic is the sheer numbers and perseverance of the invasive species. Where there's one, there's many. One worries that their numbers are infinite.

The worms cover my aunt's walkway and porch area in creating writhing piles so dense that she won't let her dog outside to go to the bathroom. The poor pup must make a mess on scraps of newspaper on her dining room. My aunt flushes the bowel movements down the drain. This is no way for a civilized person to live.

She shared pictures of this alien invasion over Thanksgiving dinner. The images ruined my appetite and continue to haunt my head. They've covered the lower half of her white exterior walls like auburn ivy, leaving a thin layer of greasy mucus as they inch higher and higher. She's pulled up floorboards in case she needs to reinforce the first-floor windows. The weight of the creatures would easily crack the single-pane glass and morph those lifeless orifices into oversized mouths continuously vomiting squirming gobs of spaghetti. It may not be long before they're wriggling out of her toilet and spigots. I pray upon His name to stop this hellish offense before such structural damage occurs.

At the onset of the attack, eradication by fire seemed like a plausible solution. My uncle went down with a blowtorch and blackened dozens of worms, but it only enveloped the area in an acrid death stench. Mustard powder and lye were used to combat the subsequent smell, as the chemicals are also supposed to irritate the skin of such devil worms.

Needless to say, the problem persisted for my poor aunt after the scorched-earth tactic failed, but the death toll continues to rise. There is no quantifiable research to back this hypothesis, but I propose that Asian jumping worms deploy a chemical communication similar to alarm pheromones whenever death is certain that becomes the revenge cry of their compatriots. The survivors, incensed by the loss of their kin, ascend from the soil and attack with even more vigor. The worms seem to multiply at an alarming rate, and the question of where exactly they came from has become less clear.

As their name indicates, they originated in Asian countries, particularly Japan, China and Korea, and have been stateside since the 19th century, but it's only been in the past decade that the Asian jumping worm has reached a new level of superiority and concern. The first reported sighting of problematic Asian jumping worms in America could be traced back to Wisconsin in 2013, at least that's what my amateur research concluded.

Within a decade, they were called a "new threat" to agriculture, according to a March 2019 article in Modern Farmer. State-sponsored outfits like the Nebraska Invasive Species Program currently keep databases on their whereabouts nationwide. In Pennsylvania, the Penn State Extension is the authority on agronomy. My aunt shared her situation, including pictures, with the top officials there. In the two years since they've been tracking Asian jumping worms in the Keystone State, her infestation is by far the worst they've seen, she shared. My aunt must fight this worm war on her own.

You see, soil becomes drier after Asian jumping worms invade, which hints at a master plan of destroying our food supply. But that may only be the start of their world domination, I fear. A rabid raccoon attacked my aunt's front door one day not long ago, which hinted at a worm-mammal alliance. My cousin hurried over and shot it dead, but a new layer had been added to the battle for my aunt's land.

The family fears locusts and frogs may be next. I told her if the creek near her driveway turns red, run, but not before leaving a trail of gasoline behind. She could easily flick a cigarette and ignite the flammable stream before making it to safety. My parents live close enough that they could see the black smoke from such a final fire and come to her aid. But for now, she must stay.

Deep in the Valley of Worms I imagine a warm womb pulsating underground, continuously growing and spawning new subterranean soldiers. This affront is no surprise, if you take a moment to think about it. Humans have been spearing worms with fishhooks and drowning them until they're eaten for centuries. Saltwater worms, including the 10-foot Bobbit worm, have adapted in becoming feared predators that prey on fish. Their peers on land may not be far behind. There's a reason why we call the deceased "worm food" and lower caskets into cement burial vaults. But what if the worms come for us on this side of six feet under? Or in our sleep?

There's a more arcane, and terrifying, worm mythos I discovered while researching obscure regional sources. In a midwestern town called Mirocaw, an annual winter solstice festival celebrates the creation of the human race, which locals believe started when a group of fallen angels molded and animated mud into the first sentient beings. But without the Supreme Creator's touch, the creatures only wailed and wallowed in the mud from which they were cast like overgrown earthworms. Eventually forced underground, these ancient Syrian abominations still exist underneath us, though yearly ritual sacrifices are necessary to keep them satisfied. If left unfed, they'll rise to feast for themselves, or so the people of Mirocaw believe.

I shudder at the thought.

It's been several weeks since my aunt shared her predicament with me. As I put all of this on the page, my throat tightens. My mouth won't stop watering, though I have no desire to eat anything but moistened dirt. The water in my glass ripples as I pick it up. I hesitate to take a sip. My stomach growls.

Asian jumping worms haven't been officially spotted in Colorado, according to experts. But what if the worms insidiously found a new carrier?

I gulp down a mouthful of water. If you're reading this, my fellow countrymen, pray for a Christmas miracle.

GRAVEYARD
GUARDIANS

I didn't notice the pavement ended under my feet until the stark surroundings shook my soul awake. I'd been walking down the street near my aunt's house. The same street my cousins and I strolled a thousand times before during the humid months of June and July, when we didn't have to worry about school and the caterpillars were busy constructing their silk moth manors in neighborhood trees.

The tiny creatures wriggled and squirmed across everybody's lawn like furry fingers at that time of year, which always irked us as kids, so we made a game of stomping them dead if they crossed our path on the road.

Being the youngest of the group, my two older cousins had to talk me into doing it, but I'd resist. I didn't want to get their gooey guts on my shoes. I'd made the mistake before, and when the caterpillar popped and splattered under my foot, the innards reminded me of green snot. At least that's what I told my cousins, but killing something so small and innocent didn't feel right. What if a giant foot from the skies snuffed us out suddenly?

But my cousins persisted, and I secretly yearned for their

approval at that age, so I became a merciless god to the neighborhood caterpillars. My only requirement was that my cousins had to cover the oblivious victims with leaves or grass first. That way I wouldn't smear them on my sole or witness the carnage I created. My cousins took turns burying the caterpillars alive, while I turned away. When they said they were finished, I'd spin back around and trample the small grave mounds flat. They'd giggle and tell me I did a good job, and then we'd proceed down the road repeating the deadly deed whenever necessary. We'd eventually make a full loop back to their house in leaving a wake of crushed insects. Years later I wondered if those poor caterpillars grew imaginary wings after the unfortunate fates they met because of me.

My mind mulled over similar questions as I wandered into the surreal cemetery at the end of the familiar road. The mansion-like mausoleums were the first sign that my world wasn't right. These weren't the quaint, two-story homes that dotted my aunt's neighborhood, but examples of the most elaborate Gothic architecture, complete with grotesque gargoyle sentries and large padlocked doors high enough to house a number of unknown leviathans.

The lawns were pocked with crumbling tombstones. Some graves were outlined with short fences, a frail attempt to keep the resident ghosts gated in. I heard faint weeping, a requiem for the recently departed, nearby. I turned to see the statue of a petrified priest. The face of the minister frozen in place as if he'd made out with Medusa.

Bouquets of long-dead roses covered the ground around me like scabs. Oak trees lined my newfound pathway like hardened arteries, their roots feeding off the barrows beneath them. Worn out shoes, each pair tied together by the shoelaces, adorned one barren tree. I stopped to observe it more. My eyes had a hard time adjusting to the sights, as the midday sun wore a veil of funeral fog, but I could still make out the crude carvings scrawled into its trunk.

"Yet we die," someone, or something, spelled out in writing that looked like a young child's.

Not far behind the tree, a dilapidated pavilion stood silent. I imagined the monsters that call this stretch of imaginary land home gathered around the wooden, circular platform to enjoy somber chamber music. My mind began to race. My chest felt tight. I started to panic, but sensed I wasn't alone and had the sudden urge to spin around. As I did, I noticed a trio of black goats standing at the line where the pavement gave way to gravel. The creature in the middle, which I presumed was the leader of the hellish herd, rushed me so quickly I barely had time to react.

It reared back on its hind legs as we locked arms in a tense caper. My body bore its weight. I felt the rigid edges of its hooves against my forearms. Should I slice the throat of this goat as a sacrifice to the arcane powers I unwittingly disturbed?

I accepted my fate and waited for the heavy boot of death. I held the gaze of the mysterious beast in forfeiture. Then it spoke without moving its mouth.

"Why are some so full of hate?" it offered.

I eased my grip and relaxed. I couldn't answer the question, but it didn't want me to. I understood it was an olive branch to a strange visitor from an even stranger place. It fell back on all fours and hurriedly trotted to rejoin the other two graveyard guardians in its original formation.

For a moment, I turned to the tree, the mournful mist lifted and painted my vision in a faint pink like streaks of blood swirling down a bathtub drain, then back, but the goats were gone.

I noticed the doors of the mausoleum mansions were now open and skeletons dressed in Victorian dresses and suits stood in the entryways with friendly faces, their mouths contorted into ghoulish grins. The dapper dead even had skeletal pets by their sides. I felt the warmth of their welcome in my bones. The high sun bathed my face. I took this as an invitation to stay as long as I'd like. I needed some time to process it all, but with a nod I assured them I'd be back. A slight breeze rustled the color-less pedals around my feet as I left the graveyard and found the recognizable road.

I don't know what I saw that particular night, or what it all means. I barely remember it, but I woke up calmer for being treated to another nocturnal dance with the brigade of black goats inside my head.

While some may waste their waking hours obsessively searching for such a new wave nightmare's origins, I'm contin-uously reminded that the world is a weird place, beyond my Earthly comprehension, if you know where to look.

ORGY OF THE SICK

The pit of possessed bodies and flailing limbs opened up and roiled before me in an instant. People pushed and pounced on each other without a second thought, a primal urge to destroy everything, and everyone, in sight the only thing on the mind of the maniacs.

A young man with a nose ring the size of a door knocker ripped his shirt off and let out a high-pitched scream that further invigorated the crazed cavity. The pulsating pit continued to grow and move like a ravenous amoeba hellbent on consuming more and more of these damned souls.

Another shirtless lunatic peered into the pit from an undisturbed corner, and then charged at an unsuspecting victim. As he rushed past, I noticed he wore a permanent pentagram on his back, seemingly etched into his skin with crude craftsmanship and watery ink. No one was safe, I thought, with demons like that among us.

A mixture of sweat, beer and blood lubricated the furious moshpit, as a devastating din of death metal played over it all. I smiled.

The 2022 Decibel Magazine Tour was responsible for the

chaotic scene at Grand Junction's Mesa Theater that night. Five bands — SpiritWorld, Enforced, Gatecreeper, Municipal Waste and Obituary — treated the near-capacity crowd to five hours of heaviness that resulted in a zombie-like display of violence that would make Dario Argento proud.

Moshing is for the young and able-bodied, so I found myself viewing the mayhem from a safe distance, though no one was impervious to spilled drinks and footless shoes that found their way outside of the pit.

I stood next to a father-and-son duo from Montrose — Dusty and Dexter — that frequently sees shows at the Mesa. Dusty and I chatted about the lineup, including opener Spirit-World, a band neither of us heard of before the tour was announced.

The Las Vegas weirdos came out dressed in pearl-snap Western shirts and cowboy hats. A honky-tonk ditty played as they took their places and strapped on their instruments. Then all hell broke loose for 30 minutes. SpiritWorld's set was comprised mostly of songs from their debut album "Pagan Rhythms," which is sprinkled with early Slayer riffage and distorted spaghetti Western yarns. They describe their sound as "death Western," and it works.

A small pit of diehard heshers began to form by the end of the first set, but the theater was still filling up, as the possessed waited for the next auditory assault.

Enforced — the crossover thrash newcomers from Richmond, Virginia — took the stage next and wasted no time blasting into their variety of razor-sharp guitars and guttural growls. The speed of Enforced's playing whipped the maniacs into a frenzy. Several people were pummeled in a push pit, but there's a moshing code — whenever someone hits the ground, stop and help them up. The band treated the audience to a heavy dose of songs from their latest record, "Kill Grid."

The pit continued to grow for Gatecreeper's performance. The new-wave death metallers from Tucson, Arizona, play music rooted in the tradition of Swedish originators Dismember and Entombed. The chainsaw guitar tone alone is enough to turn anybody into a mindless mosher, but add in vocalist Chase Mason's groans and "ughs!" and Gatecreeper has perfected the recipe for sweltering madness.

Dusty had never listened to Gatecreeper before, but was impressed by the set, which closed with fan favorite "Flamethrower," and the crowd's visceral reaction.

"This is church," I said.

"Hallelujah, I've been saved!" he replied.

Municipal Waste, also from Richmond, turned the energy up another notch in playing their beer-drenched brand of party thrash. Leadman Tony Foresta is a metal lifer, so when he says, "Open this shit up!" people listen. The pits for "Breathe Grease," "Wolves of Chernobyl" and "The Art of Partying" were so brutal that Foresta christened the Grand Junction crowd the rowdiest, and therefore the best, of the tour thus far. He even organized a wall of death, during which the headbanging zombies lined up on opposite ends of the theater without hesitation before partaking in a savage game of Red Rover whenever Foresta gave them the signal: "Alright! Fuckin' kill each other!"

There were no casualties this night, but the pit didn't fester into an endless wound until Obituary stepped onto the stage. The Tampa band is responsible for creating a gruesome subgenre — Florida death metal — and after nearly 40 years in the game, they still got it.

As the band played its intro "Redneck Stomp," I watched lead singer John Tardy prepare near the backstage door. He jumped up and down, bowed his head as if he was talking to himself, and then made the sign of the cross before running to centerstage.

Smoke and red lighting engulfed the band in a shroud of arterial spray. The pit could no longer be contained. Dusty and Dexter rushed to the front of it in an effort to stand against the stage but became lost in the sea of humanity. A hipster in a Six Feet Under long sleeve started throwing empty beer cans. Clothes were torn from torsos. The face of a man with a bloodied nose became a living Jackson Pollock painting. He shook his head, and the red liquid spread. He relished in the display of gore, licking his lips and smearing his blood across his face. This soldier of the abyss seemingly aroused a contingent of sadists. Invigorated by the sight and scent of fresh blood, more and more participants began to grope and groan.

The sonic service continued with Obituary blasting through "Final Thoughts," "Chopped in Half" and "Turned Inside Out." But the churning chasm now squirmed with pleasure, as the undead congregation reacted to the band's Southern-fried, swamp-stomping psalms.

A couple near the front of the pleasure pit shamelessly fondled one another. He wore a "Pro-fucking-pain" shirt, while hers proclaimed "Fucked by Satan," the "T" stylized as an upside down cross.

The air hung heavy with perspiration and pheromones, the sweat and spit further lubing the bacchanal. Obituary ended the frantic set with "Slowly We Rot." The pit responded in kind, continuing to revel in the debauchery and bliss of it all. I found more pleasure in watching the bedlam, relatively unscathed and unbothered, headbanging and fist-pumping along.

A small man who looked like Ronnie James Dio flashed across my face, from my left to right, before disappearing into the mass. The back of his shirt read, "Orgy of the sick."

HOUSE OF ETERNITY

Consumed by a Texas-sized labyrinth of unknown horrors and seemingly countless hallways, I stopped to retrace what led me to such a disorienting fate.

I planned to spend spring break visiting friends in Fort Worth but became lost and directionless in a modern-day House of Leaves that mimicked an antique mall shortly after my arrival. My friends had navigated the serpentine pathways before. It would be fun, they said.

I fell behind after coming across a portable Corona typewriter. I paused to peck at a few keys. "This is the end." It still worked, though it could have used a new ribbon of black ink, but the red ribbon was moist and seemed to be brand new.

The building sprawled across one city block felt larger on the inside. Texans have always boasted about how everything is bigger in Texas, but that doesn't mean everything is better. No one brags about bigger parasites, potholes or pimples.

A little boy wearing a Rangers baseball hat took my attention away from the Corona keyboard. Wide-eyed and grinning, he pressed his face against a glass case packed with pocketknives.

"I want all of them," he said to himself.

The father of the pint-sized Leatherface pulled him away.

"You already have a pocketknife," the elder butcher said.

The kid grumbled something under his breath. Pocketknives are gateway weapons to chainsaws.

Amongst the many antiquities, in the center of the maze, sat a café that bore an eerie resemblance to the one Lewis Carroll describes in "Alice's Adventures in Wonderland."

A knee-high lattice fence covered in fake ivy sectioned off the eating area, which also featured an off-kilter faux fireplace adorned with half-melted candles and topped with a funhouse mirror that rendered people who peered into it puddles of flesh, hair and eyeballs.

"Ride Like the Wind," the 1979 soft rock hit by Christopher Cross, played as I entered. I expected to be greeted by a strung-out Mad Hatter. He'd be waving an empty teacup in the air and begging patrons for more of the magic mushroom liquid he loves so much. The March Hare wouldn't be far behind. The fiends didn't seem to scare anyone off, however, as the café was bustling with business.

"If I was her, I'd use me for my skills," a girl with a mound of blonde hair on top of her head told her friend as I walked to my seat. The higher the hair the closer to heaven. At least that's what they say in Texas. After a second glance, the girl with the big hair and useful expertise was talking to a child-sized doll with an emotionless glass face and 1950s fashion sense.

The menu consisted of quiche and finger foods. I ordered an apricot iced tea first. Whenever it came, I ripped open four sugar packets and poured them into the cup, but I unexpectedly found myself in my first Texas standoff with a man at a nearby table who was stirring sugar into his sweet tea at the same time. We made eye contact and held it. The sound of our spoons twirling around the oversized plastic cups hastened. The middle-aged man wore his jet-black hair slicked back like some kitschy desperado in a Quentin Tarantino film, complete with a pencil mustache. But instead of spurs and leather, he wore a black Adidas jogging suit. What weirdos fell down the rabbit hole. I conceded and left before receiving my mushroom quiche.

A nearby bathroom offered a temporary reprieve, or so I hoped. The lime green room looked more like a mortuary, as a handful of urinals were draped in pieces of clear plastic big enough to cover bodies. A broken dentist's chair sat in one corner. An old man planted himself in front of one of the out-of-order urinals shortly after my arrival. I panicked and left without washing my hands, but not before I caught a glimpse of my reflection. A gray hair hung from my chin amongst the blackness of my beard.

After escaping the phantom pisser, a booth full of over-priced religious objects caught my attention. A six-foot cross with Jesus Christ nailed to it in eternal agony rested against the back wall. The crown of wounds adorning his skull looked fresh, but I refused to touch it to find out. Then a silver serpent slithered from the stigmatic hole in his left hand and down his smooth legs before disappearing into the top of his feet. A golden chalice gleaned atop an altar before me. A host of martyrs watched from their affixed places along the walls. I reflexively genuflected and left. A Christian cross casts a black shadow no matter which way you turn it.

Overwrought and on the brink of insanity, I stumbled upon a moth-eaten bar that could have survived the Battle of the Alamo tucked away in one of the labyrinth's far corners. Covered in a thick layer of dust, the cost put the piece out of my budget, but I was surprised to find a bartender dressed in a golden silk vest and black bowtie behind it. He asked if I needed a drink.

"Bulleit Old Fashioned," I answered.

As he started to mix my cocktail, I tried to maintain my composure and wondered to myself if the place was haunted.

"Oh, yeah," the bartender suddenly said.

"By what?"

"Well, there's a small child who runs around the front of the space, but it's harmless. Then there's Marge, who is in the men's bathroom. Toilets will randomly flush, or I'll be here by myself and go in there to find the sink is running."

"Have you ever seen anything?"

"Oh, yeah. When I first started it used to freak me out, but I have a strong sense of faith. I'll tell them that my god is stronger than your god. That seems to work."

He went on to explain that the building used to be a volunteer hospital for the poor and malnourished before a tornado rendered it a pile of splinters. The Free Masons rebuilt it as their lodge shortly after but abandoned it whenever a group of pale placid people kept disrupting their ceremonies. The supposed superior of the uninvited visitors was a tall thin man with his eyes sewn shut. Since the building evolved into the Byzantine antique mall, the unseeing patron has been spotted sporadically deep in its catacombs.

After reciting the building's history of horror, the bartender dropped a blood-red maraschino cherry in my drink and placed it on the worn wooden counter in front of me.

"On the house."

Before I could pick it up, my friend found me.

"What are you doing?"

I turned back to the cocktail and bartender, but they weren't there.

"Nothing ... just thought this was cool."

"Well, we're leaving, but we can come back another day, if you want."

"All good. I think I've seen pretty much everything I needed to."

'SOME HEADS ARE MORE HAUNTED THAN OTHERS'

I don't believe in ghosts. I don't believe in Santa Claus, the Tooth Fairy or the Easter Bunny, either. The difference, however, is that I want to believe in ghosts or some type of after-life phenomena. In my opinion, the finality of death may be something the human mind can't, or doesn't, want to fully comprehend, so we've been making up stories of friendly phantoms and tortured Earth-bound specters since we crawled from the mud and developed cognitive thought. If an undead apparition jumped out of my closet and spooked me awake in the middle of the night, I'd like to ask it some things about life A.D. Can we travel to other planets outside of our own galaxy when we die? Can ghosts even go to space (read Kurt Vonnegut's "Thanasphere")? Is it easier to lose weight post-mortem? There are too many questions to list, but I think it would be an insightful conversation.

Honestly, maybe I'm just too dumb to properly perceive spirits. My best friend, we'll call him Dale, swears he has "the vibes," which is the psychic ability to detect unexplainable presences. This power is a family trait, he's said, as one person from every generation inherits it. He's made some wild claims over the years, including blaming cow ghosts for the common, although frightening, occurrence of sleep paralysis. I didn't bother bickering with him about that one.

See, I'm weird. I actively seek out the strange and unusual, the paranormal paradoxes and "portals" to unearthly realms. For example, I recently spent a weekend in Cincinnati's Hilton Nederland Plaza hotel, which has been called the Stanley Hotel of the Queen City. For those unfamiliar, the Stanley Hotel in Estes Park was the inspiration for Stephen King's book "The Shining" after he stayed there in 1974 and dreamed that his 3-year-old son was being chased down the hotel's hallways by a firehose. It's safe to say he took some creative liberties in writing his book, but the experience clearly affected him on a deeper, psychological level.

The Nederland Plaza hotel is claimed to be the home of a chatty "lady in green" ghost that, according to most accounts, appears in an elevator, talks casually to patrons and vanishes before reaching the guest's selected floor. That, I thought to myself, would be perfect, since I did not have a date for the wedding I was attending there. As a bachelor, I've become used to not getting a plus-one to weddings, as if people think I can't find someone to accompany me to a free, over-priced party with cake.

But the lady in green would be the belle of the ball, I imagined, with her cold complexion and soulless eyes, my very own living dead girl.

The ghost in a green dress is supposedly the widow of a construction worker who died before the Art Deco hotel was opened in 1931. She eternally wanders in search of him, her true love, so the story goes.

I must have ridden the elevator 20-plus times, eagerly peering into the marble box as the doors slowly opened for a woman in a green gown.

"Excuse me, are you the lady in green?" I'd ask. Of course, she'd be surprised that I knew who she was since we never met.

"Well, yes ... I am."

"Would you care to accompany me to a wedding this evening in the Hall of Mirrors?"

She'd blush, if ghosts suffer from such a telling surge of blood flow, " ... Yes," then she'd vanish into the hotel's walls.

"Wait! Take me with you!" I'd plead. "Show me the other side. I hate weddings!"

Unfortunately, this fantasy didn't become a reality since the only people I encountered in the elevator were most definitely alive. I attended the wedding, a beautiful Jewish ceremony followed by a fun-filled reception, like I had many marriages before, alone. As the only person in the wedding party not in a serious relationship, I sat shoehorned in the corner of the head table like a ghost, barely recognized and passed over when the cordial small talk shifted to impending impregnation and accompanying nesting. The excited look in everyone's eyes made me shudder.

I glanced up at the second level, which had been completely closed off to the wedding below, and thought about the lady in green. I hoped she'd hear the liveliness of the celebration below and how funny humans were when it comes to relationships. If I crawled under the table and choked on my shrimp cocktail, no one would notice. Maybe then I could join her up there and look down on the carnival of it all. The custodians would find my body after everyone left the grand hall and call in the coroner. They'd take it away to be buried in some place I'd never been before. But it wouldn't matter. I'd still be at the Nederland in my tux with a red stain on the front of my shirt. The shrimp man and lady in green wouldn't need an official invite to future weddings at their permanent residence, but we would commit to make more public appearances, especially during the more boring services.

Sometimes reality just isn't exciting enough for me, but my experience in Cincinnati — like all ghost stories — reminded me of a quote by one of my favorite authors, Thomas Ligotti.

"There are certain fields of forces that are everywhere. And these forces, for reasons unknown to me as yet, are potentiated in some places more than others. Do you understand? The attic is not haunting your head — your head is haunting the attic. Some heads are more haunted than others, whether they are haunted by ghosts or by gods or by creatures from outer space. These are not real things. Nonetheless, they are indicative of real forces, animating and even creative forces, which your head only conceives to be some kind of spook or who knows what."

GOOD, BETTER, BEST

Like most, I tend to be a bit more reflective at the end of each of year. Maybe it's more of a modern Western practice, but I like to think back on all I've done during the previous 12 months, while keeping an eye to the next dozen. From weddings to travel, concerts and family time, I had a good and healthy 2019.

I hiked through the Arkansas Ozarks and snorkeled in the crystalline waters of the British Virgin Islands with my family. Nature's infinite beauty still calms me more than codeine.

I celebrated in Seattle as two college friends tied the knot. The mother of the groom suspected my friend Alex and I were wedding crashers, given our size and appearance. As former offensive linemen who played on the same team as the groom, she quizzed us on who we were there for upon entry. We innocently answered that we knew both the bride and the groom from school. She gave us a sideways glance and walked off. Only after the ceremony did we learn that she ran into her son's room as he prepared for his big day to tell him about the suspected intruders. We all had a good laugh about it. Congrats, Mike and Jess.

Just last week, a childhood friend who finally got around to proposing to his longtime girlfriend, asked me to be his best man. It's funny, he's told me I'd be his best man for at least 10 years, but I was still surprised when it happened. I have no idea what I'm going to say about our 20-plus years of friendship. Love ya, Lyles.

I was home for Christmas for the first time in three years and gained 15 pounds thanks to an unbalanced Italian-American diet of pasta, red sauce, chicken parmesan, meatballs and buttered bread. Thanks, Grandma.

I gave my barely legal cousin six too many shots of bourbon Christmas Eve. It's a rite of passage to get drunk with the family at some point. At least he kept his holiday ham in his stomach until he got home. Good job, Joe.

I took the year's final ride on the Harleys with my dad over the same weekend. A bond forged by horsepower and loud pipes. Ride free, pops.

I saw Slayer during their farewell tour twice and Iron Maiden for the first time with my metalhead friends. I may not remember the setlists, but I won't forget the good times. Horns.

But I'm like a shark — always moving forward. I've also already booked my first big trip of 2020 with my sister Karlee (Scandinavia — Iceland, Denmark, Sweden and Norway — in April) and have begun planning the best bachelor party ever (summertime in Telluride. Plan B: New Orleans).

I have at least 20 new books I want to read in the new year, including three about Scandinavian black metal because I'm a pseudo-anthropologist weirdo nerd when it comes to metal and its many subgenres. The Norwegians call this interest in the country's volatile and murderous scene "black packing" and even suggest things to do on the country's official tourism website, like visiting the sites of centuries old churches that were burnt to the ground in the name of teenage angst.

As for New Year's resolutions, I've never been a big fan of them. If you want to make a significant life change, do it ... like, now. Waiting for the clock to strike a certain time seems silly to me, especially when the world is constantly on different schedules. You want to lose weight and get in better shape? Great. Go outside and hike up Bear Creek every day. You want to get that tribal face tattoo you've been daydreaming about? Bold, but awesome. Book an appointment ASAP. I'm not one to judge. Acting on impulse has gotten me into plenty of trouble throughout my life — I'm sure certain people, many of whom I've left in the past, could attest to that — but that's my cross to bear, not anyone else's. Blessing to some, curse to others. No gods, no masters. If I find myself standing before the gates of eternity after dying, I won't be able to logically answer for some of my actions, especially the ones categorized as "sins" by the judges that be. If they decide to spare me from eternal hell fire, I won't be surprised if I wake up reincarnated as a butt plug. But that's my cross to bear, not anyone else's.

A friend of mine likes to say we're all works in progress. He had this epiphany a few years ago, after smoking a bowl and wandering through the city of Pittsburgh alone one night. He came across a construction site, and there it was, a literal sign, "Work in progress." The cannabinoids kicked in, and he became a modern-day mystic. Rasputin would be proud, Dave.

However you measure time and progress, one thing I'd like to suggest everyone take into consideration over these next 12 months is the idea of better. Better at empathy. Better at love and being loved. Better at picking up the phone and checking in with one another. Better at telling ones close to you how you feel about them more often. Better at accepting mistakes and learning from them. Better at humanity. We're all in this together, whether we like it or not, and there's no time like the present for change. Like the elementary school librarian, Mrs.

Cook, use to say before storytime, "Good, better, best. Never let it rest. Make your good better and your better best."

In charge of a roomful of rowdy children, she'd make us do a small exercise, like some form of juvenile yoga, before we repeated the words. We'd sit together with our legs crossed, then she'd instruct us from her chair to shake out our hands and snap our fingers twice, before folding and placing them in our lap. Staring up at her from our place on the floor, she looked like Buddha rising above us in her chair. I can't recall the stories that followed such sessions, but that last line has stayed with me over the years like the memories of 2019 and whatever events unfold during 2020 will.

GRAM AND PAP

There's a blank page staring at me, and I'm starting to feel nervous. It's waiting to be filled with words of thanks or an anecdote about Thanksgivings past. This should be easy, I initially thought, but then something strange happened, I can't seem to gather my thoughts without feeling a little melancholy. Listening to music at my desk (At The Gates, if you're wondering), I remember the last Thanksgiving with my grandma, who I called Blue Grandma at a young age because the rims of her glasses were that color, and how the whole family had dinner at our house that year. My Uncle Joe picked Gram up from the nursing home. Everyone was excited to see her, even though her health had deteriorated and left her uncommunicative and barely cognizant.

I was 16 and scared of death. Grandma wasn't doing well, and my chest felt tight that day. I didn't understand the insidious tortures of dementia, but we all talked to Grandma as if she remembered us. She didn't respond other than nodding her head or shifting her gaze, but we took it as a sign that she understood what we were saying. My eyes are starting to feel wet.

Since I can remember, my family has made a tradition of going around the Thanksgiving table and saying what we're thankful for. That year, we all included Grandma in our answers. Not long after that Grandma was gone. I remember the night she died. It was a Friday. I'd just finished a football game, whether we won or lost I can't recall, when we all went to the nursing home to meet the rest of the family. The time had come to say our goodbyes. I held Grandma's hand surprised at how light and hollow it felt. I cried. Surrounded by her children, Mum told her she could go now. That we'd be OK. Then Grandma seemingly drifted off and fell asleep for the last time.

At her funeral, Pap kept asking her why she wouldn't wake up. They had to go, he said. He had Parkinson's disease, and his mind was slowly slipping. Even after she was laid to rest, he constantly asked where his wife was. When she initially had to be moved and cared for at a facility, he would drive there and visit her every day until she went to bed.

Pap followed his wife of over 50 years by the time I turned 21. The details of his death are fuzzier, as I had been in college at the time and didn't accompany my mom to the nursing home as often as I did when Grandma was there. I didn't like going there. Sometimes I'd even wait outside when Mum would visit her mother. Such facilities are profoundly sad, like living grave-yards filled with apple sauce and "Howdy Doody" reruns. I learned this at a young age and feared them. But the older I get the more I understand why the people there griped and groaned at whoever would pay attention to them. Most were there against their will and discarded by their families. A final formality before shuffling off this mortal coil.

I miss Grandma and Pap, but I'm thankful for the time I had with them. My sister Karlee, who is 18 months younger than me, and I were recently talking about them and how we wished they were still around so we could get to know them better as adults.

Pap was a tough-as-nails World War II veteran who quit school in eighth grade to help the family financially. His hands felt like cold concrete with a handshake that could crush bones. He went on to build and manage several businesses, including a bar and restaurant named after his mother, Rose, that was a popular hangout amongst steel mill workers in Clairton, Pennsylvania. My dad, who grew up in Clairton, has worked in and around steel mills for most of his adult life. He frequented the Rose Hotel during its heyday and remembers my great-grandmother from there. Funny how the dots connect like that.

Grandma was the closest I'll ever get to a holy saint. A mother of five, she went through hell raising all those children — including my mum, Mary, who's named after her — at least that's what my aunts and uncles say. Karlee and I were the babies of the family for a while, so Grandma always watched us. She was quiet and gentle. She taught us how to play Go Fish and always carried a bag of chocolate gold coins, which I thought were real for the longest time until one melted in my pocket. She'd read to us and let us run around the backyard up until "Days of Our Lives" started. Then we'd get to pick out candy — I'd go for a full-sized Snickers bar, while Karlee usually grabbed gumdrops, Pap's favorite — and entertain ourselves.

"Like sands through the hourglass, so are the days of our lives." It feels like life happens that fast sometimes, but the memories remain. I smile.

My parents and sister are coming to Telluride for Thanksgiving this year. It's been two years since Mum and Dad were out here. Karlee visits every three months or so, for the adventure, yoga and respite, mostly. I'm thankful for them. They've always supported me, even when I decided to pick up and move across the country to this place, sight unseen, three years ago for a job. It's all worked out, and they're happy for me, but we don't see each other as often as we'd like.

There's a full page in front of me now, but I'm still not satisfied. It's really not about the word count, I tell myself, but what weight these words carry. Am I doing Grandma and Pap justice? Will anybody even read this? Will my family think I'm being a sad sap, which has become a running joke, given my apathetic disposition? I'm a Sagittarius, so I blame the cosmos, but I'm more thankful than I let on for my family and friends who continually show me love. I need to remind them of that more often.

LOVE LOST

I haven't written many love letters in my life since Taylor Ohm rejected me in the first grade. We'd met in elementary school. I didn't what love was when I scribbled, "Hey ... I love you" on a small piece of notebook paper and slid it to her in my youthful ignorance. This is how love works, I imagined back then. She immediately crumpled it up and tossed it into the trash. She was a basketball star her entire life, so she nailed the shot from her desk. Hot tears filled my eyelids. At recess I told her it was a joke. She smiled but said nothing. She didn't need to. We remained friends through high school and never spoke of my puppy love folly ever again. It was the first time I had my heart broken — better sooner than later, I suppose — but certainly not the last. Love is a messy business one doesn't necessarily have a choice in choosing, I've discovered. Even when you tell yourself you're not looking for anything, the emotion has a tendency to arise and fill your heart with fairy tales and fantasies that end with happily ever after. This Walt Disney mythos has only complicated matters.

Now, nearly 20 years later, I'm tasked with writing a love letter. "Love" has always been a weird word to me, especially when it comes to interpersonal relationships. It means different things to different people, and if those definitions don't align, a case of heartsickness quickly ensues.

Love, to me, is finding a good book on a bottom shelf at a thrift store. I once bought 10 Kurt Vonnegut books, including "Slaughterhouse-Five," for $7 at a secondhand store in Pittsburgh. As the late Indianapolis author put it: "A purpose of human life, no matter who is controlling it, is to love whoever is around to be loved."

That quote reminds me of a girl named Maria, who once told me that everyone just wants to be loved. Whenever we were spending time together, she once quipped, "You're one of those guys who likes Metallica and Pantera." Her realization meant anything between us had come to an end. No one could deny her snark. She spit it out to offend me, to get some sort of rise out of me, but I proudly replied that I am the type of guy who likes Metallica and Pantera. Once that sentence left her lips, I knew we'd never work out. I didn't even want to be friends with her after that, but she called me an "angel" before never speaking to me again. Angels have feelings, too, I told her. At least, "Master of Puppets" and "Vulgar Display of Power" will always be there for me.

Love, to me, is riding my bike — a 1974 Harley-Davidson Sportster — to nowhere in particular. There's something about being in control of your own life and death that excites me. If you've never ridden before, you won't get what I'm talking about. My pops, a burly Pittsburgh steel mill worker who taught me how to wrench and ride, calls it his therapy. Sometimes such sessions last a little longer.

Speaking of alternative therapeutic practices, a girl named Meredith used to collect the raven feathers scattered across her backyard. She'd make small trinkets that incorporated the fallen feathers like voodoo dolls. It made her feel normal, she said. I didn't say anything about that being the complete opposite of what most people consider acceptable behavior, but the truth is that I liked her definition of "normal." She wanted me to have one of these creations. This was her way of showing affection, I understood, but she moved away before giving me one. When I come across a black feather, I still think of her. Maybe her magic worked from afar after all. I haven't seen her since.

Love, to me, is metal music, a subgenre that has been mocked and scrutinized by the ignorant forever. Grateful Dead be damned, gimme Motorhead or gimme death. Born to lose, live to win.

Motorhead reminds me of a girl named Kate, who had the band's Snaggletooth mascot tattooed on her right calf. She liked to tell the story about how she ran into Motorhead's iconic frontman Lemmy in an alleyway after a show. She was relieving herself behind a trashcan during the chance encounter. Dressed in his usual cowboy boots and hat, black jeans and pearl-snap shirt, he stepped out of his limo and spotted her in the rubbish.

"Now that's rock 'n' roll," he said in his gruff voice, according to her tale. A punk rocker with a picture of Sid and Nancy in her bedroom, I imagined her and I sharing late nights and drinks at the local Owls Club where she often bartended forever. One night, when only her and I were there, we made it on the pool table in the backroom before her friend walked in and cut our session short. Billiards never been the same. She still hasn't returned my last text message.

As Lemmy once said: "Falling in love is terrible. It makes you act foolish, like an idiot. You sign your life over when you fall in love, and it's awful, it's torture. You end up walking past their house at night and looking up longingly at their window. ... Who wants to live like that?

"Women always left me because I wouldn't commit, but

then nothing changes a relationship like commitment. If you move in with someone, you lose all respect for them. All them dirty knickers on the towel rail, all that snorting and farting. Does that appeal to you? Because it doesn't to me. When you first start dating someone, it's all about being on your best behavior, and that initial magic. I never wanted the magic to stop. It's funny, isn't it? You fall in love with someone and then they try to turn you into somebody else. Why do they do that?"

BEYOND THE RAINBOW

There's a dust devil making its way down Main Street, but no one seems to notice. I stand there wondering if it's strong enough to pick me up and toss me over a rainbow to a weird place with flying death squad monkeys like Oz, or even Ouray, but it dies down and vanishes before it reaches me. I click my heels together a couple of times in an attempt to conjure the wicked winds.

"There's no place like Telluride. There's no place like Telluride," I say.

Even Mother Nature doesn't have the energy to continue during this time of year.

Watching this short burst of power recently reminds me it's offseason in Telluride. I look around to see if there are any other witnesses or winged primates, but there isn't. Of course, there's not. It's a cool April morning, and even the buildings are on vacation during this time of year. The closed signs and printed pieces of paper taped to their darkened windows carry temporary goodbye messages.

"See you in May!"

"Thanks for a wonderful winter!"

The exclamation points sarcastic middle fingers farewell.

The reopening dates differ from place to place, but the sentiment is the same — we're tired and taking a break. Whether it's vacations to far-flung places or settling into the quietness that envelops the canyon, this is the month to rest, relax, recharge and refocus before the days grow longer and the bustle of life in this corner of the mountains resumes with all its wide-eyed fervor and fury. When tornadoes of a different kind blow through with breakneck regularity.

While town's major artery is as lifeless as the agitated dirt and debris that's whipped up by a strong gust, this isn't a dirge, but a casual observation of the town many don't experience when it's sheathed in snow or serenaded with live music. The sights and sounds may not be as exciting as Gorrono's on Closing Day or a festival in Town Park, but they're still interesting, especially if you have a keen eye.

Shortly after my fantastical daydream about being caught in a whirlwind, I witness something even more magical and extraordinary, when a motorist passes me near the corner of Aspen Street. Slowing down to respect the posted speed limit, I'm shocked to see the woman shove a corndog into her mouth before resting both of her wrists on top of the steering wheel to take a selfie. Caught off guard by the detour signs, she pumps the brakes. Her head jerks forward. I let out an audible gasp. I could see in her eyes that this wasn't part of her plan. Impalement imminent, she recovers calmly and removes the corndog from her face before it's forced through the back of her head. *Dammit. What a weak payoff.*

Anyone could have viewed this mobile freakshow. I look around to see if there are any other food fetishists, but there isn't. Of course, there's not. Where she found such a perfect portable deep-fried meat product is anyone's guess, but watching someone deepthroat a corndog passes for entertainment during this time of year.

Main Street is currently receiving a facelift, and the songs of construction dominate the soundscape. The harsh hymns of a jackhammer chewing away cement. The high-pitched squeals of heavy machinery in reverse. But this concert isn't nearly as crowded as the season's last dance, an outdoor masquerade during which people dressed in pink packed themselves tight against one another to enjoy one more public display of insanity before deserting town. The audience now is a mix of orange traffic cones and signage that dots the well-used road. If only the fuddled flamingo people can see it now, their dance floor is being resurfaced before summer, and even the flags that are typically so spry and confident in their unwavering role during a busy holiday weekend lag a little lower than usual, barely rippling with the breeze.

Nearby, two skateboarders take advantage of the down time by cruising the skatepark beside the Voodoo art studios while they still can. The future site of an affordable housing project has drawn the ire and interest of many still here during this time of year, particularly those within a stone's throw of the property. The building is too high, they say. Parking will be a nightmare, too. But what about the migratory one-eyed woodpeckers that may need the airspace? These "problems" only pile up once a project of this type is proposed. But it's nothing new. There's a name for this vocal sect of locals — Nimbys. But they're not magical Munchkins eager to escort you down the Yellow Brick Road that leads to the mountainous kingdom of Telluride. Quite the opposite. It's best to leave them alone. Let them air their grievances and shake their fists at vacant lots.

But the news never sleeps. The saying makes me laugh. The number of notes we receive during this time of year to hold a story "until more people are in town" undermines our ongoing print deadlines and the timeliness of offseason happenings. The Nimbys know this is exactly what the people pulling the strings behind the curtain want. Conspiratorial government meetings are hastily organized and scheduled in order to pass nefarious plans of total and complete destruction with little to no public resistance during this time of year. The Nimbys are sure of it. Thanks for the tip, I tell them, we'll continue to cover the zaniness, as we've always done. But then again, some people still think we put out a Monday paper.

I wander into the grocery store, which is just as barren as the rest of town during this time of year, and find myself in the frozen food aisle studying all the different brands of corndogs. Maybe I'll start a new hobby this offseason. Wonder how many corndog swallowers there are on OnlyFans. I'll make my fortune virtually, then bring it live to the masses. I imagine business cards with the title "Founder of the Telluride Corndog Carnival" printed on them in big bubble letters.

I snap back to reality and catch my reflection in the glass door, my mouth hung open in an "O" big enough for one of those Ball Park jumbo wieners. I look around to see if there are any other aspiring OnlyFans models, but there isn't. Of course, there's not.

A woman in red shoes pushes past me to grab a pack of Jimmy Dean's pancakes and sausage on a stick. *Breakfast fellatio. Good idea.*

She scurries away before I have the chance to ask her if she's a good witch or bad witch.

I leave without buying anything. The sky above me is a swirl of blue and gray. Once again, I wait for a black blizzard to sweep me up and spit me out somewhere else for a while, then I can say, "We're not in Telluride anymore."

RUBATOSIS

The following is true, as far as I experienced the recent events explained within this space, which I still cannot make sense of at the time of writing this. For the past week, I've been haunted in my sleep by a demon. The malignant specter is unknown, but I am not the only eyes that have witnessed its mocking charade. My diligent duo of black cats has been similarly frightened during the nightly episodes.

The intuitive perceptiveness of felines is undeniable. It's well documented that they can sense impending death. Let one loose in a nursing home and they'll hop from lap to lap like a furry tombstone. News stories make it out to be cute, sweet even, how cats can call out when someone is going to die within a week. But the elders must fear the four-legged grim reapers. My cats apparently don't harbor such morbid powers, as they haven't helped much in my midnight crusade against the forces of evil.

It started seven days ago tomorrow with a faint beeping noise that I initially ignored as a trick of the senses, an effect of the Sandman's serenade. The sound filled every corner of the room, like a dull throbbing deep within my ears. Often coming to life at night, the cats were unbothered by the noise at first, which assuaged my initial fears. But as the prospect of slumber failed to manifest, the sound became more persistent, and louder. I counted the moments between the beeps. Thirty seconds. My heartbeat began keeping time with the weird phenomena.

I tossed and turned before sitting up in bed, as if I could spot something in the blackness. But then I saw it. The small red light on the smoke detector blinked with each beep. My pulse quickened.

The cats noticed my agitated condition. Ripley, my cat with one eye, jumped onto my chest and smothered my palpitations, which were far outpacing the unrelenting beeps by then. Bean, who still has two eyes, looked up at us from the floor beside the bed, uninterested and sluggish. He yawned and let out a faint meow from the bottom of his baby belly, then disappeared into the darkness.

Changing the battery of a smoke alarm is something one often forgets to do in the frantic activity of day-to-day life. That is until it suddenly, slowly, drives you mad during the dead of night. Only then do you think about the possibility of your domain going up in flames without warning. I may not make it out alive, but I'd at least like to know what's coming before burning.

Hadephobia began to consume me as I entered the kitchen to find a 9V battery. Digging through a drawer full of junk — empty grill lighters, expired carbon monoxide detectors, rusty right-handed scissors — I uncovered a rectangular battery with a black cat jumping through the number nine on it. "Trusted Quality," the package read. I didn't trust it. Why is this company using a cat as a mascot? The implication that I'll only lose one of my nine lives if their product fails only made my heart more agitated.

I hastily cracked open the detector attached to the ceiling and threw out the old battery, but not before touching it to my tongue. The jolt tickled my tastebuds. It still had juice. Strange, I thought. Shoving the new battery into the side slot took some extra effort as the black cat brand seemed to be bigger than the previous one with the sunglass-wearing pink rabbit but it eventually fit.

Ripley and Bean supervised my work from the floor. I returned to bed and felt my heartbeat relax. But before slipping away on my pillow, I heard another beep. This one fainter and seemingly further away.

The cats heard it, too. Three glowing eyes starred back at me, as if they were wondering what I'd do now, so I jumped out of bed and got dressed.

A friend who studies birth charts and Blood Moons once told me that you should never sleep in the nude. It only makes you more attractive to the creatures of the night.

"Don't sleep naked. However you present yourself in the physical realm, you will appear in the spirit realm. Sleeping naked is serving yourself up on a silver platter in the dreamworld. It attracts demons of lust, and you're most vulnerable when sleeping," she said.

There is no word for the fear of being found naked after a lust demon molested you to death, but I'd like to avoid it.

Cloaked in my favorite Morbid Angel hoodie and black jeans, I slowly stalked my condo, pausing every third step to listen for the insidious sound that taunted me, my heart pumping closer and closer to a fatal explosion. But hunting is a waiting game, and finding the origin has proven to be fruitless so far. Every now and then, I'll catch a shift in the shadows out of the corner of my eye. At least the cats and I are well camouflaged against this spirit in black. The new smoke detector battery promises customers nine lives. That's 27 lifetimes between the three of us, so we have that on our side. We're damn near destined to catch the night stalker.

But for now, the beeping has burrowed further into my brain with each passing night. Gaining adequate night vision and a keen sense of avoiding the hard corners of furniture have proved useful during my nocturnal pursuits. The cats can sleep through my meandering at this point, though Bean looks like a clenched fist whenever he's dreaming.

When the phantom consumes me, I'll gently place my ear on their sides and listen to their tiny hearts at work. Other than assuring myself that they're still alive, it makes my manic muscle act normal.

There is typically not one instance or event that drives a person insane. Instead the descent is a cumulation of a lifetime of small things, like dying smoke detectors and rubatosis, that push them there.

CARRION

The forest watched patiently as I struggled to reach the overlook. Smug in its mercilessness, Mother Nature is constantly the cause and witness of such human suffering. My strife isn't unique, but maybe there'd be less corpses on Mount Everest if we'd learn that we can't completely conquer the highlands.

The hike started with a steady incline and didn't level out until a bench and view of the town below offered a temporary reprieve from the trek. My summit.

Cartilage kindling popping and crackling inside my knees fueled smokeless fires. Without any water my mouthful of mucus needed emptied. Spitting over the ledge, I took the chance to sit down and ponder how small Telluride is, all alone out here, nestled into the mansion of the mountains. The barren hills this time of year reveal the scars of ski runs, a not-so-subtle reminder of man's ongoing mission to manipulate the land to his benefit, but winter wreaks its own havoc.

During summer the perch would be good high ground for putting out wildfires with a hail of hockers, I imagined. Towns-people uniting to fight the flames that destroy their homes by coughing up loogies sounds like a medieval fable. And that's why they call it Phlegm Falls, so the local legend would go.

A group of hikers joined me at the rest stop before I could completely cover the town in a cobweb of spit. I made the awkward decision to pass them on the uphill after they were visibly struggling to keep a consistent pace ahead of me.

Their faces betrayed their mountain chic outfits. Stopping every 100 feet or so, I could sense the regret. They wanted me to pass them, as if I would stop my own death march and pull them from their misery. Don't they know the trees see everything?

Panting and panicky, I became entrapped in this wilderness of mirrors. The smaller the gap between the hikers and myself became the more apprehension I could read in their body language. Tackling what they initially thought would be an easy stroll, they were now quickly falling down the food chain and facing their own mortality. The forest feasts on the weak and weary.

A firm believer that people must suffer the consequences of their decisions, I had no desire to help the poor souls, so every time they stopped to huddle under the shade of an overhanging branch or suckle on their water bottles, I stopped. My plan to maintain a respectable distance with the doomed herd didn't last long, and the space between us only lessened. Exhaustion grants humans the psychic ability to read the minds of others in a similar state. Those exerted brain waves of dismay simply cut through the air differently in the backcountry. The primal urge to play predator and prey tickled my mind. I sped up. I wasn't simply following the hikers now; I was stalking them. They sensed it, too. Brute force, not stealth, the only way to overcome them at this point. Dragging them from view of the main trail, I'd pile their carcasses in a fleshy pyramid to appease the true apex predators, an offering in asking them to grant me passage on my trek.

I made my move during one of their breaks, right before a series of switchbacks that would surely crush their spirits started, but instead of kicking their knees backwards and gnawing on their neck arteries, I nodded so hard in a friendly manner that my neck popped. They froze in shock. We didn't exchange pleasantries as I passed, only an intense glare. The prey living to die another day.

Wearing headphones and sunglasses, I've always operated under the assumption that if my senses are satisfied, then I only exist within my own head and can hike with some sort of invisibility, forgoing the formalities of enthusiastically greeting every passerby with congenial words. But it's impossible to ignore another human, no matter how aloof, in the wild.

I always feel like a fool talking to sweaty, out-of-breath strangers, reaching into my bank of canned greetings and smiling until my lips start to split.

"How's it going! Nice day!"

"Almost to the top!"

"Please, spit in my mouth! I'm parched!"

Avoiding a tail of newbies trudging along behind you like out-of-shape shadows seemed impossible on this particular day, so after fleeing the overlook and hikers I quickened my gait.

The eyes protruding from the aspens watched without winking, a freshly fallen tree resting across the trail an attempt to trip me up. Twigs cracked like bones nearby. The hunters were hungry. I should have killed those hikers. I failed them, now I'd be their main course.

The story of a Colorado trail runner killing a mountain lion with his bare hands sounded impressive until it came out that the cat he choked had been a kitten. Any bigger and it would have surely slit his throat and made spaghetti of his innards.

I pictured a beast pulling my eyeballs from their sockets like meatballs. I turned around but didn't see anything other than more bipedal beasts dressed in tight, sweat-wicking fabrics. Yoga pants might as well be sausage casings.

The hush of the breeze rustling through the leaves made the trees snicker. They're laughing at us. The woods have always been alive.

In outrunning the maniacal copse, I took a hard right onto a trail I'd never been on before. The sound of rushing water told me I couldn't be far from the waterfall where my cousin and I spread her mother's ashes a little over a year ago. I knew I had to keep moving, so with her as my guide, I followed it.

Losing my footing on a ridge near the falls, I sprawled onto all fours to avoid slipping down the gulley, the forest's eager gullet below perpetually wide open. Scrambling to my feet, bewildered and dehydrated, I slowly made my way to the base of the falls. The cool breeze welcoming my warm and worn-out body, I took off my headphones and sunglasses, before dipping my head under the strong flow of the freezing snowmelt.

I smiled and relaxed. If the forest claimed me now, I'd happily offer up my carcass as a carrion buffet for the earth and its creatures. I will not stay dead.

ACKNOWLEDGMENTS

First and foremost, I'd like to extend my gratitude to Telluride Local Media for allowing me to write and run my work in the form of The Chopping Block columns. Without such a space, who knows if any of these would even have been written and read in the first place.

Even so, this collection would certainly still be an idea in my head if it wasn't for the generous support of the Telluride Arts District, particularly its small grants program, which covered production costs and helped spread the word of the project.

Others who have helped tremendously throughout this process include cover design ace Rick Bickhart, who went above and beyond in synthesizing my zany ideas; Pat Smythe, whose eyes were instrumental in making these stories the best they could be; photographer and friend Mo Pihl for making me look more metal than I really am; and artist and friend Gordiart, a proud Ukrainian who created the cover art.

Many thanks to Schuylar Croom, the man behind the mic and lyrics for North Carolina band He Is Legend, for giving me his blessing to use the line from "That's Nasty" as an epigraph.

As stated in the dedication, my parents, Gregg and Mary, and sister, Karlee, have always supported my writing endeavors, including this book. As Karlee has said, you just have to do it. She was right, as always.

Lastly, and most importantly, to whoever is holding this, thank you for choosing to spend a moment with my madness. I hope you had as much fun reading it as I did writing it.

ABOUT THE AUTHOR

Rev. Justin Criado is an award-winning journalist and editor. The Colorado Press Association has recognized his newspaper features as some of the best in the state over the years, as he's been a writer for the past decade in Colorado, his home state of Pennsylvania and beyond.

Photo by Mo Pihl

His work has been featured in the *Denver Post*, *Westword*, *Salt Lake City Weekly*, *Phoenix New Times*, *Pittsburgh Post-Gazette* and *Pittsburgh Tribune-Review*. He's currently the editor of the *Telluride Daily Planet* newspaper in Telluride, Colorado. He can be reached at justincriado@gmail.com. Follow his never-ending nightmare on Instagram (@criado138) and Facebook.